fast-fix BAKING

BRIAN HART HOFFMAN

fast-fix BAKING

85 Recipes to Make in about 2 Hours or Less

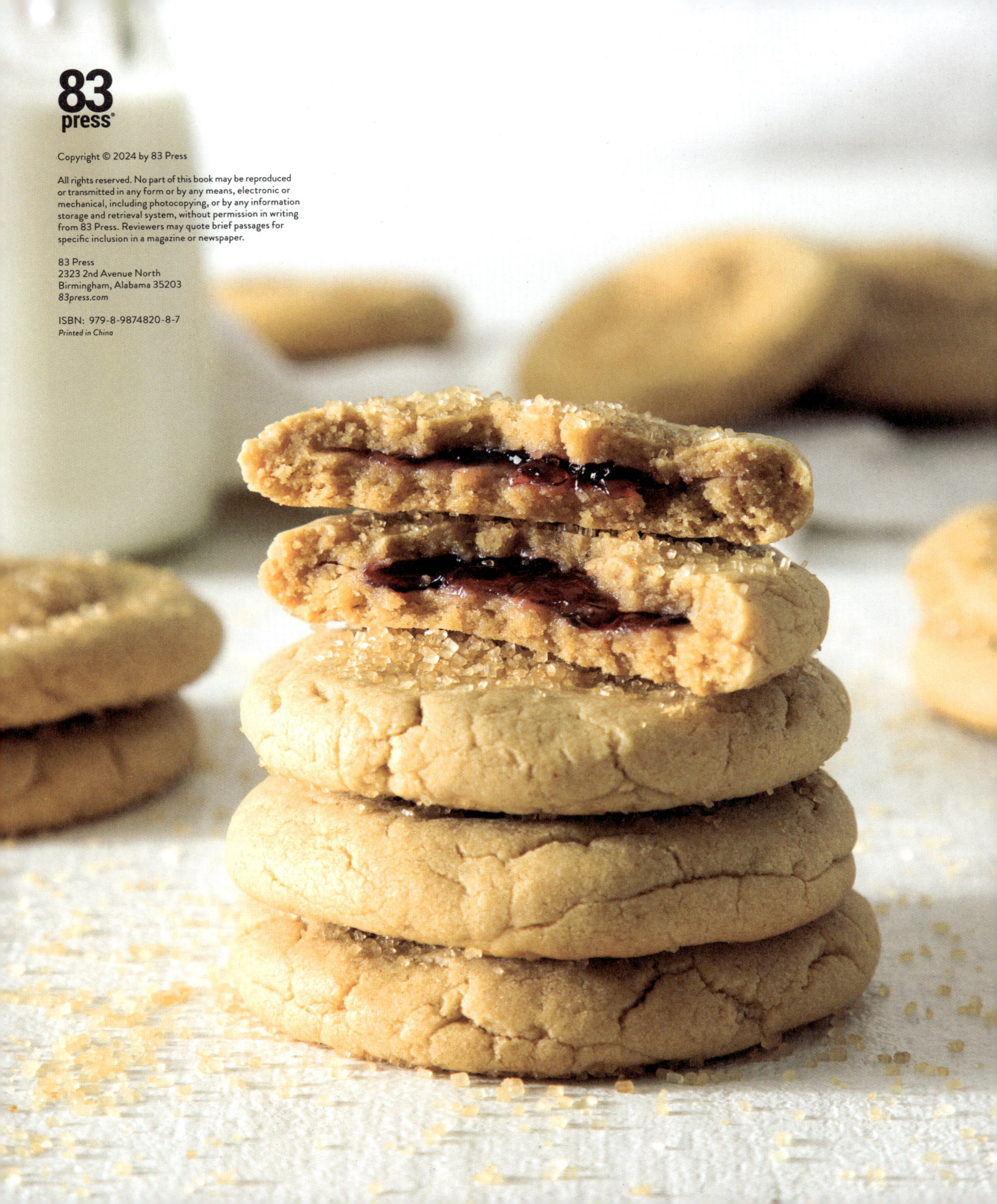

83 press

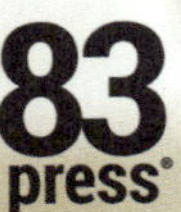

83 Press
2323 2nd Avenue North
Birmingham, Alabama 35203
83press.com

ISBN: 979-8-9874820-8-7
Printed in China

10
INTRODUCTION
Learn what makes a recipe a fast fix, plus helpful tips and tricks to get you set up for baking success

16
CAKES
Celebrate any day or every day with these fruit-filled loaves, spice-swirled Bundts, and chocolate-crowned sheet cakes

72
BREADS
Fill your daily breadbasket with these pillowy yeast rolls, buttery biscuits, tall muffins, and tender scones

120
PIES AND TARTS
Indulge in slice after slice of these hearty galettes, savory quiches, crumb-crusted pies, and meringue-topped tarts

154
COOKIES AND BARS
Find your favorite flavors and perfect textures in these cookies and bars that are guaranteed to satisfy all your cravings

bake
bake
bake
Kitchen
ARTISAN

the fast track to baking satisfaction

As much as I adore spending countless hours getting lost in a weekend baking project, there are those moments in life when I'm pressed for time in the kitchen. That's when I reach for a trusty press-in cookie crust for a pie instead of a laminated and filled pastry or a stir-together sheet cake over a lofty layered dessert. With recipes you can prep, mix, and bake in about two hours or less, these fabulous fast-fix bakes will have you and your family and friends eating well even when time is short. Each recipe in this book is filled with precise measurements, clear instructions, and beautiful photography, and I've included helpful substitutions and terrific time-saving ideas to get in the fast-fix mindset before you even begin to bake.

This splendid collection of fast-fix bakes satisfies every craving. The easy-to-make and even-easier-to-eat cakes like Dark Chocolate Sheet Cake with Peanut Butter Frosting are instant winners. I filled the "Breads" chapter with comforting recipes such as Angel Biscuits and Summer Herb Dinner Rolls. "Pies and Tarts" pages are chock-full of crunchy crumb-crusted desserts and buttery, flaky pastry-lined savory tarts, and you'll find Strawberry Thumbprint Cookies and more everyday-easy crowd-pleasers in the "Cookies and Bars" chapter.

I believe that making every ingredient earn its place is essential to minimizing effort and maximizing taste. Although these recipes are simple, they could not be further from basic; they're designed to make your baking life more enjoyable. Even when time is scarce, you can make the most out of every precious moment—by making them as delicious as possible.

happy baking!

Brian

INTRODUCTION

These fast-fix recipes are deliciously sweet and savory, straightforward, and can be made in about two hours or less.

The best part? Fast-fix recipes use everyday ingredients that are most likely in your kitchen right now, making them convenient for last-minute cravings or unexpected guests. When assembling ingredients for these fast-fix wonders, measuring by weight is the most accurate and the speediest. It eliminates the possibility of too much or not enough in your measuring cups and spoons, and you can measure ingredients directly into your mixing bowl, which means fewer dishes to clean. For those moments when you don't have the time to bring ingredients to room temperature or when you're in the middle of baking and realize you're missing a key ingredient, don't fret. My guides to ingredient substitutions and speedy shortcuts are time- and lifesavers.

emergency baking substitutions

If you don't have	*Substitute*
Apple pie spice, 1 tablespoon (6 grams)	Combine 1½ teaspoons (3 grams) ground cinnamon, ¾ teaspoon ground nutmeg, ⅜ teaspoon ground allspice, ⅛ teaspoon ground cloves, and ⅛ teaspoon ground ginger
Baking powder, 1 teaspoon (5 grams)	¼ teaspoon (1.25 grams) baking soda plus ½ teaspoon cream of tartar
Baking soda, 1 teaspoon (5 grams)	1 tablespoon (15 grams) baking powder
Brown sugar, 1 cup firmly packed (220 grams)	1 cup (200 grams) granulated sugar plus 1 tablespoon (21 grams) molasses for light or 2 tablespoons (42 grams) molasses for dark
Butter, unsalted, ½ cup (113 grams)	½ cup (113 grams) salted butter minus ¼ teaspoon salt called for in the recipe
Buttermilk, 1 cup (240 grams)	¾ cup (180 grams) plain yogurt or sour cream plus ¼ cup (60 grams) water OR ¾ cup plus 3 tablespoons (225 grams) milk plus 1 tablespoon (15 grams) distilled white vinegar or fresh lemon juice and let stand for 5 minutes before using
Cake flour, 1 cup (125 grams)	¾ cup plus 2 tablespoons (110 grams) all-purpose flour plus 2 tablespoons (16 grams) cornstarch
Cream of tartar, ¼ teaspoon	½ teaspoon (2.5 grams) fresh lemon juice
Diamond Crystal kosher salt, 1 teaspoon (3 grams)	½ teaspoon (3 grams) table salt OR ¾ teaspoon (3.5 grams) Morton kosher salt
Fresh herbs, 1 tablespoon (2 grams)	1 teaspoon (2 grams) dried herbs
Heavy whipping cream, 1 cup (240 grams)	Whisk ¾ cup (180 grams) whole milk into ¼ cup (57 grams) cooled melted unsalted butter*
Honey, 1 cup (336 grams)	1¼ cups (250 grams) granulated sugar plus ¼ cup (60 grams) water
Light corn syrup, 1 cup (336 grams)	1¼ cups (275 grams) firmly packed light brown sugar plus ⅓ cup (80 grams) water
Pumpkin pie spice, 1 tablespoon (6 grams)	Combine 1½ teaspoons (3 grams) ground cinnamon, ½ teaspoon ground ginger, ½ teaspoon ground nutmeg, ¼ teaspoon ground allspice, and ¼ teaspoon ground cloves
Self-rising flour, 1 cup (125 grams)	¾ cup (94 grams) plus 3 tablespoons (24 grams) plus 1½ teaspoons (4.5 grams) all-purpose flour plus 1½ teaspoons (7.5) grams baking powder
Semisweet chocolate, 1 ounce (30 grams)	1 ounce (30 grams) unsweetened chocolate plus 1 tablespoon (12 grams) granulated sugar
Sour cream, 1 cup (240 grams)	1 cup (240 grams) plain yogurt or ¾ cup (180 grams) buttermilk plus ¼ cup (57 grams) melted unsalted butter
Unsweetened chocolate, 1 ounce (30 grams)	3 tablespoons (15 grams) unsweetened cocoa powder plus 1 tablespoon (14 grams) vegetable oil

*This substitution is only for adding to batters and doughs; it will not whip into peaks.

1/2 CUP

warming and softening shortcuts

If you just can't wait to bake, here are a few methods to get eggs and dairy to room temperature in a flash.

EGGS

Place in-shell eggs in a bowl, and add warm (not hot) water until they're submerged. Let the eggs stand for 10 to 15 minutes—the perfect time for you to prep your baking equipment and measure your ingredients—and they should be ready to go.

BUTTER

Grate cold butter on the large holes of a box grater, or cut it into cubes and slightly separate the pieces. The smaller the pieces and the more surface area exposed, the faster the butter will soften.

MILK, BUTTERMILK, HALF-AND-HALF, AND HEAVY WHIPPING CREAM

Add the amount of dairy you need to a small saucepan, and place it over low heat. Gently swirl the pan constantly for 1 to 2 minutes to warm the liquid without overheating it.

CREAM CHEESE, SOUR CREAM, YOGURT, MASCARPONE, AND CRÈME FRAÎCHE

Fill a small saucepan with water, and heat it until it's just simmering. Add the amount of dairy you need to a heatproof bowl, and place the bowl over the saucepan, making sure the bottom of the bowl doesn't touch the water. Stir the dairy constantly for 1 to 2 minutes so it heats evenly.

A note about softening butter and dairy in the microwave: Because microwaves do not heat food evenly, you can end up with both burning-hot spots and icy-cold spots. Your best bet is to use the stovetop, but if you decide to use a microwave, go low and slow and check your ingredients frequently.

CAKES

From upside-down cakes to Bundts, rich and chocolaty to chock-full of fruit, enrobed in frosting or crowned with streusel, these easy-to-make cakes are for any and every occasion

TURTLE COFFEE CAKE

Makes 1 (9-inch) cake

Drizzled with velvety dulce de leche and studded with chopped bittersweet chocolate, this coffee cake offers the ultimate lesson in decadence. Topped with a dazzling streusel punctuated by nutty pecans, this cake brings the luscious turtle candy to the wonderful realm of coffee cakes.

2¼ cups (281 grams) all-purpose flour
⅓ cup (25 grams) Dutch process cocoa powder
2 teaspoons (4 grams) instant coffee granules
1½ teaspoons (7.5 grams) baking powder
½ teaspoon (1.5 grams) kosher salt
¼ teaspoon (1.25 grams) baking soda
1½ cups (300 grams) granulated sugar
½ cup (112 grams) vegetable oil
3 large eggs (150 grams), room temperature
1 cup (240 grams) sour cream
1½ teaspoons (6 grams) vanilla extract
4 ounces (113 grams) bittersweet chocolate, chopped
Chocolate Streusel (recipe follows)
¼ cup (75 grams) canned dulce de leche
2 to 3 tablespoons (30 to 45 grams) heavy whipping cream

1. Preheat oven to 350°F (180°C). Spray a 9-inch springform pan with baking spray with flour. Line bottom of pan with parchment paper.
2. In a medium bowl, whisk together flour, cocoa, coffee granules, baking powder, salt, and baking soda.
3. In a large bowl, whisk together sugar, oil, and eggs until combined. Whisk in sour cream and vanilla. Add flour mixture, and whisk until just combined. Fold in chopped chocolate. Spread batter into prepared pan. Firmly tap pan on a kitchen towel-lined counter to release any air bubbles. Sprinkle with Chocolate Streusel.
4. Bake until a wooden pick inserted in center comes out clean and an instant-read thermometer inserted in center registers 205°F (96°C), 1 hour and 5 minutes to 1 hour and 10 minutes. Let cool in pan for 10 minutes. Remove from pan, and place on a wire rack.
5. In a small microwave-safe bowl, heat dulce de leche and 2 tablespoons (30 grams) cream on high in 15-second intervals until dulce de leche begins to soften. Whisk until combined; add up to remaining 1 tablespoon (15 grams) cream until desired consistency is reached. Drizzle onto cake; serve warm.

Chocolate Streusel

Makes 1⅓ cups

⅓ cup (42 grams) all-purpose flour
¼ cup (50 grams) granulated sugar
2 teaspoons (4 grams) Dutch process cocoa powder
¼ teaspoon kosher salt
3 tablespoons (42 grams) unsalted butter, melted and cooled slightly
½ cup (57 grams) chopped pecans

1. In a small bowl, whisk together flour, sugar, cocoa, and salt. Whisk in melted butter until completely combined and streusel is crumbly. Stir in pecans.

CINNAMON BLUEBERRY BUNDT CAKE

Makes 1 (10-cup) Bundt cake

Blending warm cinnamon with bright blueberries, this simple cake is a Bundt-size take on a bakery-style blueberry muffin.

- **1 cup (125 grams) plus 1 tablespoon (8 grams) all-purpose flour, divided**
- **1 cup (123 grams) cake flour**
- **2 teaspoons (4 grams) ground cinnamon**
- **1 teaspoon (5 grams) baking powder**
- **1 teaspoon (3 grams) kosher salt**
- **¼ teaspoon (1.25 grams) baking soda**
- **½ cup (113 grams) unsalted butter, melted**
- **⅓ cup (67 grams) granulated sugar**
- **⅓ cup (73 grams) firmly packed light brown sugar**
- **¼ cup (85 grams) maple syrup**
- **2 large eggs (100 grams)**
- **2 teaspoons (2 grams) lemon zest (about 1 small lemon)**
- **1 teaspoon (4 grams) vanilla extract**
- **⅓ cup (80 grams) plain Greek yogurt**
- **1½ cups (210 grams) frozen blueberries**
- **Buttermilk Glaze (recipe follows)**

1. Preheat oven to 350°F (180°C).
2. In a medium bowl, whisk together 1 cup (125 grams) all-purpose flour, cake flour, cinnamon, baking powder, salt, and baking soda.
3. In a large bowl, whisk together melted butter, sugars, maple syrup, eggs, lemon zest, and vanilla. Whisk in yogurt. Add flour mixture, and whisk just until dry ingredients are moistened.
4. In a small bowl, toss together blueberries and remaining 1 tablespoon (8 grams) all-purpose flour. Fold blueberry mixture into batter.
5. Generously spray a 10-cup Bundt pan with baking spray with flour. Spread batter into prepared pan, smoothing with an offset spatula. Firmly tap pan on a kitchen towel-lined counter several times to settle batter.
6. Bake until a wooden pick inserted near center comes out clean, about 50 minutes, covering with foil halfway through baking to prevent excess browning. Let cool in pan for 15 minutes. Using a small offset spatula, gently loosen cake from center and edges of pan. Invert cake onto a wire rack, and let cool completely.
7. Spoon and spread Buttermilk Glaze onto cooled cake as desired. Refrigerate in an airtight container for up to 3 days.

Buttermilk Glaze

Makes about ⅔ cup

- **1¾ cups (210 grams) confectioners' sugar**
- **3 tablespoons (45 grams) whole buttermilk**
- **1 tablespoon (14 grams) unsalted butter, melted**
- **½ teaspoon (2 grams) vanilla extract**
- **¼ teaspoon kosher salt**

1. In a medium bowl, whisk together all ingredients until smooth. Use immediately.

APRICOT-ALMOND STREUSEL KUCHEN

Makes 1 (9-inch) cake

Inspired by a German classic, smooth and dreamy apricot preserves fill each delicate bite of this fruit and nut cake. Subtly flavored with marzipan and vanilla extract, this soft and fluffy cake is topped with sliced almonds and confectioners' sugar, making it almost as beautiful as it is tasty.

2¼ cups (282 grams) all-purpose flour, divided
1 cup (200 grams) granulated sugar, divided
¾ teaspoon (1.5 grams) kosher salt, divided
¼ cup (57 grams) cold unsalted butter, cubed
¼ cup (65 grams) marzipan or almond paste (see Note)
1 teaspoon (5 grams) tightly packed lemon zest (about 1 lemon)
¾ cup (170 grams) unsalted butter, cubed and softened
2 large eggs (100 grams), room temperature
½ teaspoon (2 grams) vanilla extract
1½ teaspoons (7.5 grams) baking powder
½ cup (120 grams) plain whole Greek yogurt, room temperature
½ cup (160 grams) apricot preserves
¼ cup (28 grams) sliced almonds
Garnish: confectioners' sugar

1. Preheat oven to 350°F (180°C). Spray a 9-inch springform pan with baking spray with flour.
2. In a small bowl, whisk together ¾ cup (94 grams) flour, ¼ cup (50 grams) granulated sugar, and ¼ teaspoon salt. Using a pastry blender or 2 forks, cut in cold butter and marzipan or almond paste until well combined and mixture is crumbly. Refrigerate for at least 30 minutes or until ready to use.
3. In the bowl of a stand mixer, whisk together lemon zest and remaining ¾ cup (150 grams) granulated sugar. Add softened butter; using the paddle attachment, beat at medium speed until creamy, about 3 minutes, stopping to scrape sides of bowl. Add eggs, one at a time, beating until combined after each addition. Beat in vanilla.
4. In a medium bowl, whisk together baking powder, remaining 1½ cups (188 grams) flour, and remaining ½ teaspoon (1.5 grams) salt. With mixer on medium-low speed, gradually add baking powder mixture to sugar mixture alternately with yogurt, beginning and ending with baking powder mixture, beating until just combined after each addition. Spread batter into prepared pan. Run a knife or wooden pick through batter, and firmly tap pan on a kitchen towel-lined counter to release any air bubbles. Using a knife or offset spatula, carefully spread preserves over surface of batter. Sprinkle streusel evenly onto preserves; top with almonds.
5. Bake until top is golden brown and a wooden pick inserted in center comes out clean, 55 minutes to 1 hour, covering with foil to prevent excess browning if necessary. Let cool in pan for 10 minutes. Remove from pan, and garnish with confectioners' sugar, if desired. Serve warm.

Note: *Marzipan/almond paste can omitted from the streusel if desired; increase butter to ½ cup (113 grams), and add ½ teaspoon (2 grams) almond extract and an additional 2 tablespoons (24 grams) granulated sugar.*

PEANUT BUTTER-BANANA UPSIDE-DOWN CAKE

Makes 1 (10-inch) cake

Rich, tender peanut butter cake meets caramelized bananas in this sweet spin on an upside-down cake. A layer of halved bananas is nestled into a simple caramel, where they'll take on a caramelized flavor all their own as the sugars in the bananas bake. The final flip out of the pan reveals gooey caramel, beautifully caramelized bananas, and a fluffy cake that'll be impossible to resist.

- ½ cup (113 grams) plus ⅓ cup (76 grams) unsalted butter, softened and divided
- ⅔ cup (147 grams) firmly packed light brown sugar
- 1 tablespoon (15 grams) fresh lemon juice
- 3 large firm bananas (225 grams), halved lengthwise
- 1 cup (200 grams) granulated sugar
- 2 large eggs (100 grams), room temperature
- ¾ cup (192 grams) creamy peanut butter
- 1 teaspoon (4 grams) vanilla extract
- 1½ cups (188 grams) all-purpose flour
- 1 teaspoon (5 grams) baking powder
- ¼ teaspoon (1.25 grams) baking soda
- ¼ teaspoon kosher salt
- ½ cup (120 grams) whole milk

1. Preheat oven to 350°F (180°C).
2. In a 10-inch cast-iron skillet, melt ⅓ cup (76 grams) butter over medium heat. Whisk in brown sugar, and cook, stirring occasionally, until mixture starts to caramelize, 4 to 5 minutes. Whisk in lemon juice until combined. Remove from heat. Place banana halves, cut side down, on top of caramel, cutting bananas to fit if necessary.
3. In the bowl of a stand mixer fitted with the paddle attachment, beat granulated sugar and remaining ½ cup (113 grams) butter at medium speed until fluffy, 3 to 4 minutes, stopping to scrape sides of bowl. Add eggs, one at a time, beating well after each addition. Beat in peanut butter and vanilla until combined.
4. In a medium bowl, whisk together flour, baking powder, baking soda, and salt. With mixer on low speed, gradually add flour mixture to butter mixture alternately with milk, beginning and ending with flour mixture, beating just until combined after each addition. Gently spread batter onto bananas in skillet, smoothing top with an offset spatula.
5. Bake until a wooden pick inserted in center comes out clean and an instant-read thermometer inserted in center registers 205°F (96°C), 45 to 50 minutes. Let cool in skillet for 10 minutes. Carefully invert cake onto a rimmed serving plate. Serve warm. Refrigerate in an airtight container for up to 2 days.

COFFEE AND CREAM MARBLED COFFEE CAKE

Makes 1 (9-inch) cake

Enriched with bittersweet chocolate and espresso, this sweetly swirled cake will take your morning beverage to new, delightful heights. Espresso Streusel adorns the top of this rich cake, adding a textured crunch to each bite.

1¼ cups (284 grams) unsalted butter, softened
2¼ cups (450 grams) granulated sugar
5 large eggs (250 grams), room temperature
1 tablespoon (13 grams) vanilla extract
3 cups (375 grams) all-purpose flour
2½ teaspoons (12.5 grams) baking powder
1 teaspoon (3 grams) kosher salt
¾ cup (180 grams) sour cream, room temperature
3 ounces (85 grams) bittersweet chocolate, melted and cooled slightly
3 tablespoons (21 grams) instant espresso powder
Espresso Streusel (recipe follows)

1. Preheat oven to 350°F (180°C).
2. In the bowl of a stand mixer fitted with the paddle attachment, beat butter and sugar at medium speed until fluffy, 3 to 4 minutes, stopping to scrape sides of bowl. Add eggs, one at a time, beating well after each addition. Beat in vanilla.
3. In a medium bowl, whisk together flour, baking powder, and salt. With mixer on low speed, add flour mixture to butter mixture in three additions alternately with sour cream, beginning and ending with flour mixture, beating just until combined after each addition. Divide batter in half (about 3 cups or 780 grams each).
4. In a small bowl, stir together melted chocolate and espresso powder until espresso fully dissolves. Add to 1 portion of batter, and fold until combined. Leave remaining portion of batter as is.
5. Using 2 (1½-tablespoon) spring-loaded scoops, scoop batters in an alternating pattern into bottom of a 9-inch nonstick tube pan. (See Note.) Firmly tap pan on a kitchen towel-lined counter 2 to 3 times to help level batter and fill pan. Create another layer with alternating cake batters. Tap pan again. Scoop remaining batter randomly on top. Using a butter knife, swirl batters together in a figure eight motion. Tap pan again to help level batter and fill in any gaps. Sprinkle Espresso Streusel on top, breaking up large chunks.
6. Bake until a wooden pick inserted in center comes out clean, about 1 hour and 5 minutes, loosely covering with foil to prevent excess browning, if necessary. Let cool in pan for 20 minutes. Remove from pan. Serve warm.

Note: *Using a regular tube pan will work; you just need to spray it first with baking spray with flour. The bake time remains the same, but the edges will be lightly crisp. Do not use a tube pan with a removable bottom; batter will leak out.*

ESPRESSO STREUSEL

Makes about 1 cup

⅔ cup (83 grams) all-purpose flour
⅓ cup (67 grams) granulated sugar
1 tablespoon (7 grams) instant espresso powder
¼ teaspoon kosher salt
¼ cup (57 grams) cold unsalted butter, cubed

1. In a medium bowl, whisk together flour, sugar, espresso powder, and salt. Using a pastry blender or 2 forks, cut in cold butter until combined and mixture is crumbly. Mix with your hands until mixture resembles wet sand. Freeze until ready to use.

STIR-TOGETHER CHOCOLATE CAKE WITH CHOCOLATE BUTTERCREAM

Makes 1 (8-inch) cake

This indulgent, craving-conquering chocolate cake can be mixed and baked in less than an hour. Dutch process cocoa delivers an intense but not bitter chocolate flavor, and oil and sour cream keep the cake moist and tender for days. The generous spread of buttercream frosting makes a good thing even better!

---

1 cup (125 grams) all-purpose flour
1 cup (220 grams) firmly packed light brown sugar
¾ teaspoon (3.75 grams) baking soda
¼ teaspoon kosher salt
½ cup (120 grams) hot coffee or hot water
⅓ cup (25 grams) Dutch process cocoa powder
⅓ cup (80 grams) sour cream
¼ cup (56 grams) vegetable oil
1 teaspoon (4 grams) vanilla extract
1 large egg (50 grams)
Chocolate Buttercream (recipe follows)
Garnish: chocolate curls and shavings

1. Preheat oven to 350°F (180°C). Spray an 8-inch round cake pan with baking spray with flour; line bottom of pan with parchment paper.
2. In a large bowl, whisk together flour, sugar, baking soda, and salt.
3. In a medium bowl, whisk together hot coffee or hot water and cocoa until smooth and well combined. Whisk in sour cream, oil, and vanilla until well combined. Whisk in egg until smooth. Whisk cocoa mixture into flour mixture just until no white streaks remain. Spread batter into prepared pan.
4. Bake until a wooden pick inserted in center comes out with a few moist crumbs, 30 to 35 minutes. Let cool in pan for 10 minutes. Remove from pan, and let cool completely on a wire rack.
5. Spread Chocolate Buttercream onto cooled cake. Garnish with chocolate, if desired. Store in an airtight container for up to 3 days.

Chocolate Buttercream

Makes about 3½ cups

1 cup (227 grams) unsalted butter, softened
2½ cups (300 grams) confectioners' sugar
½ cup (43 grams) Dutch process cocoa power
¼ teaspoon kosher salt
2½ tablespoons (38 grams) heavy whipping cream
½ teaspoon (2 grams) vanilla extract

1. In the bowl of a stand mixer fitted with the paddle attachment, beat butter at low speed until smooth and creamy, about 1 minute.
2. In a medium bowl, sift together confectioners' sugar, cocoa, and salt. With mixer on low speed, add sugar mixture to butter alternately with cream, beating until smooth after each addition, stopping to scrape paddle and bottom and sides of bowl. Beat in vanilla. Increase mixer speed to medium-high, and beat until light and fluffy, about 2 minutes. Use immediately.

SWEET POTATO SPICE CAKE WITH TOASTED MERINGUE

Makes 1 (9-inch) cake

This fall stunner is ready to impress with a generous amount of golden-hued sweet potato and fluffy peaks of meringue topping!

¾ cup (170 grams) unsalted butter, softened
1¼ cups (250 grams) granulated sugar
¾ cup (165 grams) firmly packed light brown sugar
2 large eggs (100 grams), room temperature
1½ cups (365 grams) mashed cooked sweet potato (see Note)
2½ teaspoons (10 grams) vanilla extract
2¼ cups (281 grams) all-purpose flour
2 teaspoons (10 grams) baking powder
1½ teaspoons (3 grams) ground cinnamon
½ teaspoon (2.5 grams) baking soda
½ teaspoon (1.5 grams) kosher salt
½ teaspoon (1 gram) ground ginger
½ teaspoon (1 gram) ground black pepper
¾ cup (180 grams) whole buttermilk, room temperature
Swiss Meringue (recipe follows)

1. Preheat oven to 350°F (180°C). Spray a 9-inch square baking pan with baking spray with flour. Line pan with parchment paper, letting excess extend over two sides of pan.
2. In the bowl of a stand mixer fitted with the paddle attachment, beat butter and sugars at medium speed until fluffy, 3 to 4 minutes, stopping to scrape sides of bowl. Add eggs, one at a time, beating well after each addition. Add sweet potato and vanilla, and beat just until combined.
3. In a medium bowl, whisk together flour, baking powder, cinnamon, baking soda, salt, ginger, and pepper. With mixer on low speed, gradually add flour mixture to butter mixture alternately with buttermilk, beginning and ending with flour mixture, beating until just combined after each addition. Spread batter into prepared pan.
4. Bake until a wooden pick inserted in center comes out clean, 1 hour and 5 minutes to 1 hour and 10 minutes. Let cool completely in pan on a wire rack.
5. Using excess parchment as handles, remove cooled cake from pan. Top with Swiss Meringue as desired. Using a handheld kitchen torch, carefully brown meringue. Serve immediately. Store in an airtight container for up to 2 days.

Note: *Scrub 2 large sweet potatoes and prick all over with a fork. Microwave on high, turning every 2 minutes, until a sharp knife can easily be inserted in the center. Halve potatoes lengthwise, and let cool completely, cut side up. Peel potatoes and mash flesh smooth before measuring. Mashed flesh freezes well in a heavy-duty resealable plastic bag; let it thaw completely before using.*

Swiss Meringue

Makes about 5 cups

1½ cups (300 grams) granulated sugar
5 large egg whites (150 grams), room temperature
2 tablespoons (42 grams) light corn syrup
¾ teaspoon (2.25 grams) kosher salt
½ teaspoon (1 gram) cream of tartar
1½ teaspoons (6 grams) vanilla extract

1. In the top of a double boiler, whisk together sugar, egg whites, corn syrup, salt, and cream of tartar. Cook over simmering water, stirring occasionally, until a candy thermometer registers 140°F (60°C).
2. Transfer mixture to the bowl of a stand mixer fitted with the whisk attachment. Beat at high speed until mixture has cooled and tripled in volume, 5 to 7 minutes. Beat in vanilla. Use immediately.

STICKY TOFFEE PUDDING

Makes 1 (9-inch) cake

This cake is decadent and intricately sweet from dates and molasses-rich brown sugar. A more-than-generous drizzle of sauce is the final flourish for this gloriously indulgent dessert.

1¼ cups (250 grams) pitted dates, coarsely chopped
¾ cup (180 grams) water
1¼ cups (275 grams) firmly packed light brown sugar
½ cup (113 grams) unsalted butter, softened
3 tablespoons (63 grams) golden syrup (see Note)
2 large eggs (100 grams), room temperature
1 teaspoon (4 grams) vanilla extract
2 cups (250 grams) all-purpose flour
1½ teaspoons (7.5 grams) baking powder
¾ teaspoon (2.25 grams) kosher salt
½ teaspoon (1 gram) ground cloves
¼ teaspoon ground ginger
½ teaspoon (2.5 grams) baking soda
Toffee Sauce (recipe follows)

1. Preheat oven to 350°F (180°C). Spray a 9-inch square baking pan with baking spray with flour. Line pan with parchment paper, letting excess extend over sides of pan.
2. In a medium saucepan, bring dates and ¾ cup (180 grams) water to a boil over medium-high heat. Reduce heat to medium, and cook, stirring frequently, until dates are softened and most of water is absorbed, about 5 minutes. Using an immersion blender, purée mixture until smooth. (Alternatively, transfer mixture to the work bowl of a food processor, and pulse until smooth.)
3. In the bowl of a stand mixer fitted with the paddle attachment, beat brown sugar, butter, and golden syrup at medium speed until combined, 1 to 2 minutes. Add eggs, one at a time, beating well after each addition. Beat in vanilla.
4. In a medium bowl, whisk together flour, baking powder, salt, cloves, and ginger. With mixer on low speed, add half of flour mixture, beating until just combined.
5. Stir baking soda into warm date mixture, and immediately add to sugar mixture; beat at low speed until combined. Beat in remaining flour mixture, stopping to scrape bottom and sides of bowl. Spoon batter into prepared pan, smoothing with an offset spatula.
6. Bake until pudding springs back when lightly touched in center and a wooden pick inserted in center comes out with a few moist crumbs, 45 to 50 minutes. Let cool in pan for 10 minutes. Using excess parchment as handles, remove from pan, and let cool for 10 minutes on a wire rack. Serve warm with Toffee Sauce.

Note: *Golden syrup is an essential ingredient in many British desserts. It's thick and amber-colored, with a uniquely buttery, caramellike flavor. Although it's likely not stocked in your local grocery store, it's easy to find online.*

Toffee Sauce

Makes 1⅔ cups

¼ cup (57 grams) unsalted butter
¾ cup (165 grams) firmly packed light brown sugar
¼ teaspoon kosher salt
1 cup (240 grams) heavy whipping cream

1. In a medium saucepan, melt butter over medium heat. Whisk in brown sugar and salt. Add cream; increase heat to medium-high, and bring to a boil, whisking until sugar dissolves. Cook, stirring constantly, until mixture begins to thicken and an instant-read thermometer registers 220°F (104°C) to 230°F (110°C). Let cool slightly. Serve warm.

MANGO SOUR CREAM CAKE

Makes 1 (8-inch) cake

This quickly assembled cake makes a decadent treat when you can get your hands on a wonderfully ripe golden-hued mango. It tastes as bright and sunny as a summer day.

¾ cup (170 grams) unsalted butter, softened
1 cup (200 grams) granulated sugar
2 large eggs (100 grams), room temperature
2 teaspoons (8 grams) vanilla extract, divided
1¾ cups (219 grams) all-purpose flour
1 teaspoon (5 grams) baking powder
½ teaspoon (1.5 grams) kosher salt
¼ teaspoon (1.25 grams) baking soda
¼ cup (60 grams) sour cream, room temperature
3 tablespoons (45 grams) whole milk, room temperature
1¼ cups (175 grams) diced peeled mango
1½ cups (180 grams) confectioners' sugar
2 tablespoons (30 grams) fresh lime juice
Garnish: diced peeled mango

1. Preheat oven to 350°F (180°C). Spray a tall-sided 8-inch round cake pan with baking spray with flour. Line bottom of pan with parchment paper.

2. In the bowl of a stand mixer fitted with the paddle attachment, beat butter and granulated sugar at medium speed until pale and fluffy, 3 to 4 minutes, stopping to scrape sides of bowl and paddle. Add eggs, one at a time, beating until combined after each addition. Beat in 1 teaspoon (4 grams) vanilla.

3. In a medium bowl, whisk together flour, baking powder, salt, and baking soda. In a small bowl, whisk together sour cream and milk. With mixer on low speed, gradually add flour mixture to butter mixture alternately with sour cream mixture, beginning and ending with flour mixture, beating until just combined after each addition and stopping to scrape sides of bowl and paddle. Using a rubber spatula, gently stir in mango. Spread batter into prepared pan.

4. Bake until a wooden pick inserted in center comes out with a few moist crumbs, 50 to 55 minutes, covering with foil during final 10 minutes of baking to prevent excess browning. Let cool in pan on a wire rack for 10 minutes. Remove from pan, and let cool completely on a wire rack.

5. In a small bowl, whisk together confectioners' sugar, lime juice, and remaining 1 teaspoon (4 grams) vanilla. Pour onto cooled cake. Garnish with mango, if desired. Let stand until glaze is set, about 15 minutes. Refrigerate in an airtight container for up to 3 days.

CONFETTI SNACK CAKE

Makes 1 (8-inch) cake

Topped with a crumbly and delicious sprinkles-filled streusel and baked to golden perfection, this butter-based cake will be your new go-to for any time of day. Whether you're looking for a sweet treat to go with your afternoon coffee or an unbeatable dessert after dinner, this rainbow-colored delight will make every snack feel like a celebration!

⅓ cup (76 grams) unsalted butter, room temperature
½ cup (100 grams) granulated sugar
3 tablespoons (42 grams) firmly packed light brown sugar*
2 large eggs (100 grams), room temperature
4 teaspoons (24 grams) vanilla bean paste, divided
1½ cups (188 grams) all-purpose flour
1 teaspoon (5 grams) baking powder
¾ teaspoon (2.25 grams) kosher salt
¼ teaspoon (1.25 grams) baking soda
½ cup (120 grams) plus 2 tablespoons (30 grams) whole milk, divided
⅓ cup (30 grams) quins (see Note)
Confetti Streusel (recipe follows)
1 cup (120 grams) confectioners' sugar
1 tablespoon (14 grams) unsalted butter, melted

1. Preheat oven to 350°F (180°C). Spray an 8-inch square baking pan with baking spray with flour. Line pan with parchment paper, letting excess extend over sides of pan.
2. In the bowl of a stand mixer fitted with the paddle attachment, beat room temperature butter, granulated sugar, and brown sugar at medium speed until light and fluffy, 3 to 4 minutes, stopping to scrape sides of bowl. Add eggs, one at a time, beating until combined after each addition and stopping to scrape sides of bowl. Beat in 2 teaspoons (12 grams) vanilla bean paste.
3. In a medium bowl, whisk together flour, baking powder, salt, and baking soda. With mixer on low speed, gradually add flour mixture to butter mixture alternately with ½ cup (120 grams) milk, beginning and ending with flour mixture, beating until just combined after each addition. Gently fold in sprinkles until combined. Pour batter into prepared pan, smoothing top. Top with Confetti Streusel.
4. Bake until a wooden pick inserted in center comes out clean, 30 to 40 minutes. Let cool in pan for 10 minutes. Using excess parchment as handles, remove from pan, and let cool completely on a wire rack.
5. In a small bowl, whisk together confectioners' sugar, melted butter, remaining 2 tablespoons (30 grams) milk, and remaining 2 teaspoons (12 grams) vanilla bean paste. Drizzle glaze onto cake. Store in an airtight container for up to 3 days.

Note: *Quins are sometimes called sequins or confetti sprinkles.*

CONFETTI STREUSEL

Makes about 1¼ cups

½ cup (63 grams) all-purpose flour
¼ cup (50 grams) granulated sugar
¼ teaspoon kosher salt
3 tablespoons (42 grams) unsalted butter, melted
2 tablespoons (12 grams) rainbow sprinkles

1. In a small bowl, whisk together flour, sugar, and salt. Add melted butter; using a rubber spatula, work in butter until mixture is crumbly. Fold in sprinkles. Refrigerate for at least 30 minutes before using.

SICILIAN WHOLE ORANGE CAKE

Makes 1 (8-inch) cake

I love that this cake uses the entire fruit, peel and all, and it's so tender that it practically melts in your mouth! After flavoring the batter with fresh orange juice and fruity olive oil, I brush the baked cake with tangy orange syrup and top with orange slices so it stays moist and citrusy from the first slice to the very last bite.

---

2 Valencia oranges (400 grams), chopped and seeded (leave peel on)
1¾ cups (219 grams) all-purpose flour
1 cup (96 grams) finely ground almond flour
2 teaspoons (10 grams) baking powder
¼ teaspoon kosher salt
1½ cups (300 grams) granulated sugar, divided
3 large eggs (150 grams), room temperature
½ cup (112 grams) olive oil
1 teaspoon (4 grams) vanilla extract
¼ cup (60 grams) fresh orange juice
Garnish: orange slices

1. Preheat oven to 350°F (180°C). Spray a 3-inch-tall 8-inch round cake pan with baking spray with flour. Line pan with parchment paper; spray parchment.
2. In the work bowl of a food processor, process chopped oranges until almost completely puréed, about 30 seconds. (There should still be some small chunks remaining.)
3. In a medium bowl, whisk together flours, baking powder, and salt.
4. In the bowl of a stand mixer fitted with the whisk attachment, beat 1¼ cups (250 grams) sugar and eggs at medium-high speed until pale and thick, 5 to 7 minutes. With mixer on medium speed, add oil and vanilla, beating until combined. Add puréed orange, beating until completely combined. Add flour mixture, and beat at low speed just until combined, stopping to scrape sides of bowl. Spread batter into prepared pan.
5. Bake until top is golden and a wooden pick inserted in center comes out clean, about 1 hour and 15 minutes, loosely covering with foil after 45 minutes of baking to prevent excess browning. Let cool in pan for 10 minutes.
6. Meanwhile, in a small saucepan, heat orange juice and remaining ¼ cup (50 grams) sugar over medium heat, whisking occasionally, until sugar dissolves, about 5 minutes.
7. Remove warm cake from pan, and place on a wire rack. Brush orange syrup onto cake. Let cool completely on wire rack. Garnish with orange slices, if desired. Store in an airtight container for up to 3 days.

MIXED BERRY RICOTTA CAKE

Makes 1 (9-inch) cake

My friend Jessie Sheehan created this wonderfully moist and tender cake. An extra egg yolk adds extra moisture, and thick and creamy yet mild-in-flavor ricotta is the perfect addition to this "summer in a cake pan" treat. More than a cup of mixed berries is added to the oil-based batter in stages to prevent berry sinkage. A final sprinkling of turbinado sugar provides a little crunchy texture and sparkly shimmer to a cake that will likely become one of your favorites.

- 1¼ cups (250 grams) granulated sugar
- ½ cup (112 grams) vegetable oil
- 2 teaspoons (8 grams) vanilla extract
- 2 large eggs (100 grams)
- 1 large egg yolk (19 grams)
- 1¼ cups (276 grams) whole-milk ricotta cheese
- 1 teaspoon (5 grams) baking powder
- ¼ teaspoon (1.25 grams) baking soda
- ½ teaspoon (1.5 grams) kosher salt
- 1½ cups (188 grams) all-purpose flour
- 9 ounces (255 grams) assorted fresh berries (such as blueberries, raspberries, and strawberries), chopped if large
- Turbinado sugar, for sprinkling
- Garnish: confectioners' sugar

1. Preheat oven to 350°F (180°C). Spray a 9-inch round cake pan with cooking spray. Line bottom of pan with parchment paper.

2. In a large bowl, whisk together granulated sugar, oil, and vanilla until well combined. Add eggs and egg yolk, one at a time, whisking until combined after each addition. Add ricotta, baking powder, baking soda, and salt, one at a time, whisking until combined after each addition. Using a rubber spatula, gently stir in flour just until last streak of flour is absorbed. Spread half of batter (about 475 grams) into prepared pan. Top with half of berries. Gently spread remaining batter onto berries in pan. Sprinkle with turbinado sugar and remaining berries.

3. Bake until a wooden pick inserted in center comes out clean, 55 minutes to 1 hour and 5 minutes, rotating pan after 30 minutes of baking and covering with foil during final 15 minutes of baking to prevent excess browning. Let cool in pan on a wire rack for 10 minutes. Remove from pan, and let cool completely on a wire rack. Garnish with confectioners' sugar before serving, if desired.

pro tip

To get this cake to the table in the blink of an eye, freeze it until it's just barely warm after removing it from the pan, about 20 minutes.

RASPBERRY OLIVE OIL CAKE

Makes 1 (8-inch) cake

This cake is all about the simple joys of baking. Made divinely tender with olive oil and boasting a crunchy sugar topping, this one-layer wonder hides tender bursts of raspberry within.

- ¾ cup (150 grams) granulated sugar
- 3 large eggs (150 grams)
- ½ cup (112 grams) extra-virgin olive oil
- ½ cup (120 grams) whole milk
- 1 teaspoon (4 grams) vanilla extract
- 1¾ cups (219 grams) plus 1 tablespoon (8 grams) all-purpose flour, divided
- ¾ teaspoon (2.25 grams) kosher salt
- ½ teaspoon (2.5 grams) baking powder
- ¼ teaspoon (1.25 grams) baking soda
- 1¼ cups (160 grams) frozen raspberries
- 3 tablespoons (36 grams) turbinado sugar

1. Preheat oven to 350°F (180°C). Spray an 8-inch round cake pan with baking spray with flour. Line bottom of pan with parchment paper.

2. In the bowl of a stand mixer fitted with the whisk attachment, beat granulated sugar and eggs at high speed until mixture begins to thicken and pale, about 2 minutes. With mixer on high speed, add oil in a slow, steady stream, beating until combined. Add milk and vanilla, beating until combined.

3. In a medium bowl, whisk together 1¾ cups (219 grams) flour, salt, baking powder, and baking soda. With mixer on low speed, gradually add flour mixture to sugar mixture, beating just until combined and stopping to scrape sides of bowl.

4. In a small bowl, carefully stir together raspberries and remaining 1 tablespoon (8 grams) flour until completely coated; fold raspberry mixture into batter. Spread batter into prepared pan. Sprinkle turbinado sugar evenly on top.

5. Bake until a wooden pick inserted in center comes out clean and an instant-read thermometer inserted in center registers 205°F (96°C), 45 to 50 minutes. Let cool in pan for 10 minutes. Remove from pan, and let cool completely on a wire rack. Store in an airtight container at room temperature for up to 3 days.

Note: *Other berries can be used in place of raspberries. Just make sure the berries aren't too large, or are cut smaller, so they don't sink to the bottom of the cake.*

IRISH COFFEE COFFEE CAKE

Makes 1 (9-inch) cake

Behold, a nightcap coffee cake. Buzzing with espresso and packed with two layers of whiskey-spiked streusel, this cake is a tender delicacy you'll enjoy to the last crumb.

½ cup (113 grams) unsalted butter, softened
1 cup (200 grams) granulated sugar
2 large eggs (100 grams), room temperature
2 cups (250 grams) all-purpose flour
1¼ teaspoons (6.25 grams) baking powder
½ teaspoon (2.5 grams) baking soda
½ teaspoon (1.5 grams) kosher salt
⅔ cup (160 grams) whole buttermilk
⅓ cup (80 grams) Irish whiskey
3 tablespoons (18 grams) espresso powder, divided
1 teaspoon (4 grams) vanilla extract
½ teaspoon (2 grams) coffee extract
Irish Whiskey Streusel (recipe follows)
Espresso sugar (see Note), to serve

1. Preheat oven to 350°F (180°C). Spray a 9-inch square baking pan with cooking spray. Line pan with parchment paper, letting excess extend over sides of pan.
2. In the bowl of a stand mixer fitted with the paddle attachment, beat butter and granulated sugar at medium speed until fluffy, about 2 minutes, stopping to scrape sides of bowl. Add eggs, one at a time, beating well after each addition.
3. In a medium bowl, whisk together flour, baking powder, baking soda, and salt. In a liquid-measuring cup, whisk together buttermilk, whiskey, 2 tablespoons (12 grams) espresso powder, and extracts until espresso dissolves. With mixer on low speed, gradually add flour mixture to butter mixture alternately with buttermilk mixture, beginning and ending with flour mixture, beating just until combined after each addition.
4. Spoon half of batter into prepared pan, spreading with an offset spatula. Sprinkle with half of Irish Whiskey Streusel and remaining 1 tablespoon (6 grams) espresso powder. Top with remaining batter, gently spreading with an offset spatula and making sure streusel doesn't blend with batter too much. Crumble remaining Irish Whiskey Streusel onto batter, squeezing to form clumps.
5. Bake until a wooden pick inserted in center comes out clean, 40 to 45 minutes. Let cool on a wire rack for 30 to 45 minutes. Sprinkle with espresso sugar, if desired. Serve warm. Store in an airtight container for up to 3 days.

Note: *To make espresso sugar, process together 1 cup (200 grams) granulated sugar and 1 tablespoon (6 grams) espresso powder in the work bowl of a food processor until well combined and uniform in color.*

Irish Whiskey Streusel

Makes 3 cups

1¾ cups (219 grams) all-purpose flour
1 cup (220 grams) firmly packed light brown sugar
2 teaspoons (4 grams) espresso powder
1¼ teaspoons (2.5 grams) ground cinnamon
½ teaspoon (1.5 grams) kosher salt
½ cup plus 2 tablespoons (141 grams) cold unsalted butter, cubed
1 tablespoon (15 grams) Irish whiskey

1. In the work bowl of a food processor, pulse flour, brown sugar, espresso powder, cinnamon, and salt until combined. Add cold butter and whiskey, and pulse until pea-size clumps of streusel form, about 10 times. Refrigerate until ready to use.

CINNAMON SWIRL BUNDT

Makes 1 (10-cup) Bundt cake

Rich vanilla and cinnamon batters swirl together to create this showstopping Bundt cake. With pieces of a beloved cinnamon-sugar cereal crushed and mixed into both batters and a drizzle on top, I don't blame you if this cake becomes both a breakfast and a dessert staple.

1¼ cups (284 grams) unsalted butter, softened
2 cups (400 grams) granulated sugar
5 large eggs (250 grams), room temperature
1¾ cups (219 grams) plus 2 tablespoons (16 grams) unbleached cake flour, divided
1 cup (93 grams) very finely ground crunchy cinnamon square cereal (see Note)
1½ teaspoons (4.5 grams) kosher salt
½ teaspoon (2.5 grams) baking soda
½ cup (120 grams) sour cream, room temperature
⅓ cup (80 grams) whole milk, room temperature
1 tablespoon (13 grams) vanilla extract
2½ tablespoons (15 grams) ground cinnamon
Creamy Milk Glaze (recipe follows)
Garnish: crunchy cinnamon square cereal

1. Preheat oven to 325°F (170°C).
2. In the bowl of a stand mixer fitted with the paddle attachment, beat butter and sugar at medium-low speed just until combined; increase mixer speed to medium, and beat until fluffy, 3 to 4 minutes, stopping to scrape sides of bowl. Add eggs, one at a time, beating until well combined after each addition and stopping to scrape sides of bowl. (Mixture may look a bit broken at this point, but batter will come together.)
3. In a large bowl, whisk together 1¾ cups (219 grams) flour, ground cereal, salt, and baking soda. In a medium bowl, whisk together sour cream, milk, and vanilla. With mixer on low speed, gradually add flour mixture to butter mixture alternately with sour cream mixture, beginning and ending with flour mixture, beating just until combined after each addition and stopping to scrape sides of bowl. Transfer half of batter (about 3 cups or 714 grams) to another medium bowl; add cinnamon, folding until well combined. Fold remaining 2 tablespoons (16 grams) flour into remaining batter in mixer bowl.
4. Spray a 10-cup Bundt pan with baking spray with flour. Spoon and spread about one-third of plain batter (about 1 cup or 230 grams) in bottom of prepared pan; top with one-third of cinnamon batter (about 1 cup or 230 grams), spreading into an even layer. Repeat procedure twice with remaining batters. Tap pan on a kitchen towel-lined counter a few times to settle batter and release any air bubbles.
5. Bake for 45 minutes. Rotate pan, and cover with foil; bake until a wooden pick inserted near center comes out clean and an instant-read thermometer inserted near center registers at least 200°F (93°C), 15 to 20 minutes more. Let cool in pan for 10 minutes. Using a small offset spatula, loosen cake from center of pan. Invert cake onto a wire rack, and let cool completely.
6. Transfer cooled cake to a serving plate. Spoon Creamy Milk Glaze over and into grooves of cake. Garnish with cereal, if desired.

Note: *I ground the cereal to a fine powder or flour-like consistency using a spice grinder and then sifted it using a fine-mesh sieve before measuring. This recipe will still work if there are larger pieces of cereal, but these tend to have a chewy texture when baked.*

Creamy Milk Glaze

Makes about ¾ cup

1¾ cups (210 grams) confectioners' sugar
3 tablespoons (45 grams) whole milk
1½ tablespoons (22.5 grams) sour cream
¼ teaspoon kosher salt

1. In a medium bowl, whisk together all ingredients until smooth and well combined. Use immediately.

CANNOLI SHEET CAKE

Makes 1 (13x9-inch) cake

Studded with dark chocolate chunks and topped with a fluffy ricotta frosting, this sheet cake is a delicate, soft take on the crunchy Italian classic.

1¾ cups (385 grams) firmly packed light brown sugar
¾ cup (170 grams) unsalted butter, melted
3 large eggs (150 grams)
1 tablespoon (13 grams) vanilla extract
3 cups (375 grams) all-purpose flour
1 tablespoon (15 grams) baking powder
1 teaspoon (5 grams) baking soda
1 teaspoon (3 grams) kosher salt
1½ cups (360 grams) whole buttermilk
1 cup (170 grams) chopped bittersweet chocolate
Whipped Ricotta Frosting (recipe follows)
Garnish: chopped chocolate, chopped pistachios

1. Preheat oven to 350°F (180°C). Line a 13x9-inch baking pan with parchment paper, letting excess extend over sides of pan.
2. In a large bowl, stir together brown sugar and melted butter until combined. Add eggs and vanilla, stirring until well combined.
3. In a medium bowl, whisk together flour, baking powder, baking soda, and salt. Gradually add flour mixture to sugar mixture alternately with buttermilk, beginning and ending with flour mixture, stirring just until combined after each addition. Stir in chocolate. Spread batter into prepared pan.
4. Bake until a wooden pick inserted in center comes out clean, 40 to 45 minutes. Let cool in pan for 15 minutes. Using excess parchment as handles, remove from pan, and let cool completely on a wire rack.
5. Spread Whipped Ricotta Frosting onto cake. Garnish with chocolate and pistachios, if desired. Cover and refrigerate for up to 3 days.

Whipped Ricotta Frosting

Makes about 6 cups

¾ cup (169 grams) whole-milk ricotta cheese (see Note)
2 ounces (55 grams) cream cheese, softened
1 tablespoon (15 grams) fresh orange juice
½ teaspoon (2 grams) vanilla extract
¼ teaspoon kosher salt
2 cups (240 grams) confectioners' sugar
2 cups (480 grams) cold heavy whipping cream

1. In the work bowl of a food processor, pulse ricotta, cream cheese, orange juice, vanilla, and salt until completely smooth, about 1 minute. Transfer to a large bowl; whisk in confectioners' sugar.
2. In the bowl of a stand mixer fitted with the whisk attachment, beat cream at medium-high speed until stiff peaks form. Fold whipped cream into ricotta mixture in three additions. Use immediately, or cover and refrigerate until ready to use.

Note: *It's important to use high-quality, full-fat ricotta cheese so it will not split when creating the frosting.*

PEAR FRITTER LOAF CAKE

Makes 1 (9x5-inch) loaf cake

While the fritter may be most associated with the apple, the succulent pear lends itself equally well to the crisp and cakey fritter frontier. Loaded with spices, fresh pear, and smooth vanilla bean seeds, this fritter-turned-loaf cake is a delectable welcome for one of fall's favorite flavors.

⅔ cup (133 grams) granulated sugar
⅔ cup (146 grams) firmly packed light brown sugar, divided
½ cup plus 2 tablespoons (140 grams) neutral oil
½ cup (120 grams) sour cream, room temperature
¼ cup (60 grams) water, room temperature
2 large eggs (100 grams), room temperature
1½ teaspoons (9 grams) vanilla bean paste
2½ cups (313 grams) plus 1 teaspoon (3 grams) all-purpose flour, divided
2 teaspoons (10 grams) baking powder
1 teaspoon (3 grams) kosher salt
½ teaspoon (1 gram) ground nutmeg
¼ teaspoon (1.25 grams) baking soda
1 cup (151 grams) ½-inch-chopped Bartlett pears (about 1 medium pear), divided
2½ teaspoons (5 grams) ground cinnamon, divided
Vanilla Glaze (recipe follows)

1. Preheat oven to 350°F (180°C). Spray a 9x5-inch loaf pan with cooking spray. Line pan with parchment paper, letting excess extend over sides of pan.
2. In a large bowl, whisk together granulated sugar, ⅓ cup (73 grams) brown sugar, oil, sour cream, ¼ cup (60 grams) room temperature water, eggs, and vanilla bean paste.
3. In a medium bowl, whisk together 2½ cups (313 grams) flour, baking powder, salt, nutmeg, and baking soda. Gradually add flour mixture to sugar mixture, stirring just until barely combined.
4. In a small bowl, toss together ¾ cup (113 grams) pears, 1 teaspoon (2 grams) cinnamon, and remaining 1 teaspoon (3 grams) flour. Add pear mixture to batter; fold just until combined and no flour pockets remain.
5. In another small bowl, stir together remaining ⅓ cup (73 grams) brown sugar and remaining 1½ teaspoons (3 grams) cinnamon.
6. Spoon half of batter (about 532 grams) into prepared pan, smoothing into an even layer. Sprinkle with half of brown sugar mixture. Top with remaining batter and remaining ¼ cup (38 grams) pears, lightly pressing pears into batter. Sprinkle with remaining brown sugar mixture. Using a butter knife, fold and swirl brown sugar mixture into top of batter as desired. (Pan will be quite full, but batter will not overflow.)
7. Bake until a wooden pick inserted in center comes out clean, 1 hour and 10 minutes to 1 hour and 20 minutes, rotating pan halfway through baking and loosely covering with foil after 35 minutes of baking to prevent excess browning. Let cool in pan for 10 minutes. Remove from pan, and let cool completely on a wire rack.
8. Drizzle Vanilla Glaze onto cooled cake. Cover and refrigerate for up to 3 days.

VANILLA GLAZE

Makes about ½ cup

1⅓ cups (160 grams) confectioners' sugar
¼ teaspoon (1.5 grams) vanilla bean paste
1½ to 2 tablespoons (22.5 to 30 grams) water

1. In a medium bowl, stir together confectioners' sugar and vanilla bean paste. Gradually whisk in 1½ to 2 tablespoons (22.5 to 30 grams) water until desired consistency is reached. Use immediately.

HONEY-ALMOND CAKE

Makes 1 (8-inch) cake

This honeyed cake is perfect for marking Rosh Hashanah, the Jewish New Year, or the end of a crisp autumn night. Almonds, ginger, and honey are the main flavors, while applesauce and sour cream help create a supremely tender crumb.

- ½ cup (113 grams) unsalted butter, softened
- 1 cup (200 grams) granulated sugar
- 2 large eggs (100 grams), room temperature
- 6 tablespoons (126 grams) honey, divided
- ¼ teaspoon (1 gram) almond extract
- 1¼ cups (156 grams) all-purpose flour
- ¾ cup (72 grams) superfine almond flour
- 2 teaspoons (10 grams) baking powder
- 2 teaspoons (6 grams) kosher salt
- 1 teaspoon (2 grams) ground ginger
- ¾ cup (180 grams) unsweetened applesauce
- ⅓ cup plus 1 tablespoon (95 grams) whole milk, room temperature
- ⅓ cup (80 grams) sour cream, room temperature
- 1 tablespoon (15 grams) fresh lemon juice
- ¼ cup (28 grams) sliced almonds, toasted

1. Preheat oven to 350°F (180°C). Spray an 8-inch round cake pan with baking spray with flour. Line bottom and sides of pan with parchment paper.

2. In the bowl of a stand mixer fitted with the paddle attachment, beat butter and sugar at medium speed until fluffy, 3 to 4 minutes, stopping to scrape sides of bowl. Add eggs, one at a time, beating well after each addition. Beat in 2 tablespoons (42 grams) honey and almond extract.

3. In a medium bowl, whisk together flours, baking powder, salt, and ginger. In another medium bowl, whisk together applesauce, milk, sour cream, and lemon juice. With mixer on low speed, gradually add flour mixture to butter mixture alternately with applesauce mixture, beginning and ending with flour mixture, beating just until combined after each addition. Pour batter into prepared pan, smoothing top with an offset spatula.

4. Bake until lightly golden and a wooden pick inserted in center comes out with just a few moist crumbs, 45 to 50 minutes. Let cool in pan for 15 minutes. Remove from pan, and let cool completely on a wire rack.

5. In a small microwave-safe bowl, heat remaining 4 tablespoons (84 grams) honey on high in 10-second intervals, stirring between each, until thin and pourable. Spoon honey onto cake, and sprinkle with almonds. Store in an airtight container for up to 2 days, or refrigerate in an airtight container for up to 5 days. If refrigerating, let come to room temperature before serving.

CARROT-PUMPKIN CAKE

Makes 1 (9-inch) cake

A marriage between two orange-hued favorites, carrot and pumpkin, this well-spiced cake brings plenty of seasonal charm to the table. Aromatic toasted pecans and a rich cream cheese frosting round out the simple perfection of this autumnal stunner.

1¼ cups (250 grams) granulated sugar
1 cup (244 grams) canned pumpkin
½ cup (112 grams) canola oil
2 large eggs (100 grams), room temperature
1 teaspoon (6 grams) vanilla bean paste
1¾ cups (219 grams) all-purpose flour
1½ teaspoons (3 grams) ground cinnamon
1 teaspoon (5 grams) baking powder
¾ teaspoon (2.25 grams) kosher salt
½ teaspoon (2.5 grams) baking soda
½ teaspoon (1 gram) ground ginger
½ teaspoon (1 gram) ground nutmeg
1½ cups (161 grams) lightly packed grated carrots
½ cup (57 grams) finely chopped toasted pecans
Spiced Cream Cheese Frosting (recipe follows)
Garnish: finely chopped toasted pecans

1. Preheat oven to 350°F (180°C). Spray a 9-inch springform pan with baking spray with flour. Line bottom of pan with parchment paper.
2. In a large bowl, whisk together sugar, pumpkin, oil, eggs, and vanilla bean paste.
3. In a medium bowl, whisk together flour, cinnamon, baking powder, salt, baking soda, ginger, and nutmeg. Gradually add flour mixture to sugar mixture, stirring just until combined. Fold in carrots and pecans just until combined. Spread batter into prepared pan.
4. Bake until a wooden pick inserted in center comes out clean, 40 to 45 minutes. Let cool in pan for 15 minutes. Remove sides of pan, and let cool completely on pan base on a wire rack.
5. Using a serrated knife, level top of cooled cake, if desired.
6. Spoon 1 cup (265 grams) Spiced Cream Cheese Frosting into a pastry bag fitted with a ½-inch French star piping tip (Ateco #866). Spread remaining Spiced Cream Cheese Frosting on top and sides of cake. Using frosting in bag, pipe swirls around top edge of cake. Garnish with pecans, if desired. Refrigerate in an airtight container for up to 5 days.

Spiced Cream Cheese Frosting

Makes about 4 cups

12 ounces (340 grams) cream cheese, softened
⅔ cup (150 grams) unsalted butter, softened
½ teaspoon (1 gram) ground cinnamon
½ teaspoon (2 grams) vanilla extract
¼ teaspoon ground nutmeg
¼ teaspoon ground ginger
5 cups (600 grams) confectioners' sugar

1. In the bowl of a stand mixer fitted with the paddle attachment, beat cream cheese and butter at medium speed until smooth and creamy, about 1 minute. Add cinnamon, vanilla, nutmeg, and ginger, and beat until combined. With mixer on low speed, gradually add confectioners' sugar, beating until combined; increase mixer speed to medium, and beat until smooth and fluffy, about 2 minutes. Use immediately.

CLASSIC VANILLA POUND CAKE

Makes 1 (10-cup) Bundt cake

This perfectly sweet and buttery pound cake is the definition of simple satisfaction.

- 1½ cups (340 grams) unsalted butter, softened
- 2 cups (400 grams) granulated sugar
- 6 large eggs (300 grams), room temperature
- 1 tablespoon (13 grams) vanilla extract
- 3 cups (375 grams) all-purpose flour
- 1 teaspoon (3 grams) kosher salt
- ½ teaspoon (2.5 grams) baking powder
- 1 cup (240 grams) whole milk, room temperature

1. Preheat oven to 350°F (180°C).

2. In the bowl of a stand mixer fitted with the paddle attachment, beat butter and sugar at medium speed until fluffy, 5 to 7 minutes, stopping to scrape sides of bowl. Reduce mixer speed to low. Add eggs, one at a time, beating well after each addition. Beat in vanilla.

3. In a medium bowl, whisk together flour, salt, and baking powder. With mixer on low speed, gradually add flour mixture to butter mixture alternately with milk, beginning and ending with flour mixture, beating just until combined after each addition.

4. Spray a 10-cup Bundt pan with baking spray with flour. Pour batter into prepared pan. Firmly tap pan on kitchen towel-lined counter to settle batter.

5. Bake until a wooden pick inserted near center comes out clean, about 1 hour. Let cool in pan for 10 minutes. Remove from pan, and let cool completely on a wire rack.

pro tip

For flavor variations, substitute 1½ teaspoons (6 grams) almond extract for vanilla extract or 1 tablespoon (3 grams) lemon zest for vanilla extract; add lemon zest with butter and sugar.

VANILLA APPLESAUCE CAKE

Makes 1 (9-inch) cake

Applesauce gives this cake its tender crumb and tart apple notes, and a double dose of vanilla adds a rich, floral flavor. There is a generous amount of frosting for this cake, which can easily be halved if you prefer.

---

2 cups (250 grams) all-purpose flour
2 teaspoons (10 grams) baking powder
2 teaspoons (4 grams) ground cinnamon
1 teaspoon (3 grams) kosher salt
½ teaspoon (2.5 grams) baking soda
½ teaspoon (1 gram) ground ginger
¼ teaspoon ground cloves
1 cup (200 grams) granulated sugar
1 cup (240 grams) unsweetened applesauce
½ cup (120 grams) whole buttermilk, room temperature
½ cup (112 grams) vegetable oil
2 large eggs (100 grams)
1 teaspoon (4 grams) vanilla extract*
Vanilla Bean Frosting (recipe follows)

1. Preheat oven to 350°F (180°C). Line bottom of a 9-inch springform pan with parchment paper; lightly spray sides of pan with baking spray with flour.
2. In a large bowl, whisk together flour, baking powder, cinnamon, salt, baking soda, ginger, and cloves.
3. In a medium bowl, whisk together sugar, applesauce, buttermilk, oil, eggs, and vanilla. Fold sugar mixture into flour mixture until well combined. Spread batter into prepared pan.
4. Bake until a wooden pick inserted in center comes out clean, 35 to 40 minutes. Let cool in pan for 10 minutes. Remove from pan, and let cool completely on a wire rack.
5. Spread Vanilla Bean Frosting onto cooled cake. Store in an airtight container for up to 3 days.

Vanilla Bean Frosting

Makes about 4 cups

1 (8-ounce) package (226 grams) cream cheese, softened
½ cup (113 grams) unsalted butter, softened
4 cups (480 grams) confectioners' sugar
1 tablespoon (18 grams) vanilla bean paste*
½ teaspoon (1.5 grams) kosher salt

1. In the bowl of a stand mixer fitted with the paddle attachment, beat cream cheese at medium-low speed until smooth, about 2 minutes. Add butter, and beat until smooth, about 2 minutes. Add confectioners' sugar, 1 cup (120 grams) at a time, beating well after each addition. Increase mixer speed to medium-high. Add vanilla bean paste and salt. Increase mixer speed to medium-high, and beat for 2 minutes. Use immediately.

**I used Heilala Pure Vanilla Extract and Pure Vanilla Paste.*

TORTA DI SUSINE

Makes 1 (9-inch) cake

This cake celebrates the allure and flavor of fresh plums and encapsulates the Italian ideal that excellent ingredients should be presented simply and beautifully.

- 2 large eggs (100 grams), room temperature
- ¾ cup (150 grams) granulated sugar
- ½ cup (112 grams) neutral oil
- ½ cup (120 grams) whole milk, room temperature
- 2 teaspoons (12 grams) vanilla bean paste
- 2 cups (250 grams) unbleached cake flour
- 2 teaspoons (10 grams) baking powder
- ½ teaspoon (1.5 grams) kosher salt
- 2 small plums (220 grams) (any varietal), halved and sliced ¼ inch thick

1. Preheat oven to 325°F (170°C). Spray a 9-inch springform pan with baking spray with flour. Line bottom of pan with parchment paper.

2. In the bowl of a stand mixer fitted with the whisk attachment, beat eggs at high speed until uniform in color and foamy, about 1 minute. With mixer on medium speed, add granulated sugar in a slow, steady stream, beating until combined. Increase mixer speed to high, and beat until thick and pale, about 2 minutes. With mixer on medium-low speed, add oil in a slow, steady stream, beating until combined; scrape sides of bowl. With mixer on medium speed, gradually add milk and vanilla bean paste, beating until combined.

3. In a medium bowl, whisk together flour, baking powder, and salt. Fold flour mixture into egg mixture just until combined. Pour batter into prepared pan. Gently tap pan on a kitchen towel-lined counter to release any large air bubbles. Top with plum slices, going all the way to edges and overlapping as needed.

4. Bake until a wooden pick inserted in center comes out with a few moist crumbs, 45 to 55 minutes. Let cool in pan for 15 minutes. Remove sides of pan, and let cool on a wire rack for 30 minutes. Serve warm. Store in an airtight container for up to 3 days.

CITRUS CHIFFON CAKE

Makes 1 (10-inch) cake

First dreamed up by Californian Harry Baker, chiffon cake is famous for its lighter-than-air texture. This fluffy base works wonderfully with a kiss of citrus, such as lemon, lime, or orange. Using all three gives this cake a decidedly sunny disposition.

1½ cups (300 grams) granulated sugar, divided
1 tablespoon (12 grams) tightly packed orange zest
1 tablespoon (5 grams) packed lemon zest
2 teaspoons (3 grams) packed lime zest
2¼ cups (281 grams) unbleached cake flour
1 tablespoon (15 grams) baking powder
1 teaspoon (3 grams) kosher salt
7 large eggs (350 grams), separated and room temperature
½ cup (112 grams) vegetable oil
½ cup (120 grams) fresh orange juice
¼ cup (60 grams) fresh lemon juice
1 teaspoon (4 grams) vanilla extract
½ teaspoon (2 grams) cream of tartar
Citrus Glaze (recipe follows)

1. Preheat oven to 350°F (180°C).
2. In a large bowl, stir together 1 cup (200 grams) sugar and zests until well combined. Whisk in flour, baking powder, and salt.
3. In the bowl of a stand mixer fitted with the whisk attachment, beat egg yolks at medium-high speed until doubled in volume, about 3 minutes. Reduce mixer speed to medium, and add oil in a slow, steady stream, beating until combined. Reduce mixer speed to low, and add orange juice, lemon juice, and vanilla, beating until combined. Transfer to another large bowl.
4. Clean bowl of stand mixer and whisk attachment. Using the whisk attachment, beat egg whites and cream of tartar at medium speed until soft peaks form, about 2 minutes. With mixer on low speed, add remaining ½ cup (100 grams) sugar in a slow, steady stream, beating until combined. Increase mixer speed to medium-high, and beat until medium-soft peaks form, about 2 minutes.
5. Using a balloon whisk, gradually fold flour mixture into egg yolk mixture until combined. Fold egg white mixture into egg yolk mixture in three additions. Pour batter into a 10-inch removable-bottom tube pan. Gently run a knife through batter to release any air bubbles.
6. Bake until golden brown and a wooden pick inserted near center comes out clean, about 55 minutes. Immediately invert pan (onto a bottle if needed; see Note), and let cool completely.
7. Using an offset spatula, loosen cooled cake from sides and bottom of pan. Remove from pan, and transfer to a cake plate. Pour Citrus Glaze all over cake. Store in an airtight container for up to 3 days.

Note: *If your pan doesn't have prongs to support it, rest it on the narrow neck of a full glass bottle, like a wine bottle. You turn the pan upside down to ensure that your freshly baked cake doesn't sink as it cools.*

CITRUS GLAZE

Makes about 1½ cups

2 cups (240 grams) confectioners' sugar
2 tablespoons (30 grams) fresh orange juice
1 tablespoon (15 grams) fresh lemon juice

1. In a medium bowl, whisk together all ingredients until smooth. Use immediately.

STRAWBERRY CREAM CAKE

Makes 1 (6-cup) cake

I soaked a vanilla sponge cake with simple syrup before blanketing it in layers of creamy whipped mascarpone and fresh, juicy strawberries.

---

1 cup (200 grams) granulated sugar, divided
¼ cup (60 grams) water
1½ cups (188 grams) cake flour
1 teaspoon (2 grams) ground cardamom
½ teaspoon (2.5 grams) baking powder
½ teaspoon (1.5 grams) kosher salt
½ cup (113 grams) unsalted butter, room temperature (see Notes)
2 large eggs (100 grams), room temperature
1½ teaspoons (6 grams) vanilla bean paste
½ cup (120 grams) heavy whipping cream, room temperature
Whipped Mascarpone Topping (recipe follows)
Garnish: fresh strawberries

1. Preheat oven to 350°F (180°C). Spray a 6-cup charlotte cake pan (see Notes) with baking spray with flour.
2. In a small saucepan, heat ¼ cup (50 grams) sugar and ¼ cup (60 grams) water over medium heat until sugar dissolves. Remove from heat, and let cool completely.
3. In a medium bowl, combine flour, cardamom, baking powder, and salt.
4. In the bowl of a stand mixer fitted with the paddle attachment, beat butter, eggs, vanilla bean paste, and remaining ¾ cup (150 grams) sugar at medium speed until combined, 1 to 2 minutes, stopping to scrape sides of bowl. (Mixture will look broken, but batter will come together.) With mixer on low speed, add flour mixture alternately with cream, beginning and ending with flour mixture, beating just until combined after each addition. Scrape sides of bowl; increase mixer speed to medium, and beat just until batter is smooth and combined, 15 to 30 seconds. Spread batter in prepared pan; tap pan on a kitchen towel-lined counter to settle batter and release any air bubbles. Using a small offset spatula, spread batter so edges are ¼ inch higher than center.
5. Bake until edges are lightly golden and a wooden pick inserted in center comes out clean, 22 to 30 minutes. Let cool in pan for 10 minutes. Remove from pan. Brush with simple syrup, and let cool completely on a wire rack.
6. Fill center of cooled cake with strawberry Whipped Mascarpone Topping, smoothing with an offset spatula. Top with remaining Whipped Mascarpone Topping. Garnish with strawberries, if desired.

Notes: *Unlike softened butter, room temperature butter should provide no resistance when pressed with a finger.*

I used a Nordic Ware Charlotte Cake Pan. A 6-cup round cake pan can be used if you do not have a charlotte pan.

Dollop and spread plain and strawberry Whipped Mascarpone Topping onto cake as desired, or serve with fresh berries alongside cake slices.

Whipped Mascarpone Topping

Makes 4 cups

1 cup (130 grams) fresh sliced strawberries
½ cup (100 grams) granulated sugar, divided
1 cup (225 grams) mascarpone cheese, softened
1½ cups (360 grams) heavy whipping cream

1. In a medium bowl, stir together strawberries and ¼ cup (50 grams) sugar. Let stand until juices are extracted and sugar dissolves, 30 to 40 minutes, stirring occasionally.
2. In the work bowl of a food processor, process strawberry mixture until smooth.
3. In a large bowl, whisk mascarpone until smooth.
4. In the bowl of a stand mixer fitted with the whisk attachment, beat cream at medium-high speed until frothy. Add remaining ¼ cup (50 grams) sugar, 1 tablespoon (12 grams) at a time, beating until medium-stiff peaks form. Whisk whipped cream mixture into mascarpone in three additions. Transfer 1½ cups (219 grams) whipped mascarpone to another medium bowl; add strawberries, and whisk vigorously just until thickened to original consistency. (Do not overmix.) Use immediately.

DARK CHOCOLATE SHEET CAKE WITH PEANUT BUTTER FROSTING

Makes 1 (13x9-inch) cake

With a generous slather of creamy frosting on a fudgy cake, this classic pairing of chocolate and peanut butter is the ultimate indulgence.

- 4 ounces (115 grams) semisweet chocolate, chopped
- 6 tablespoons (84 grams) unsalted butter
- 1½ cups (360 grams) water
- 1 cup (200 grams) granulated sugar
- 1 cup (220 grams) firmly packed light brown sugar
- ¼ cup (21 grams) unsweetened cocoa powder
- ⅔ cup (160 grams) sour cream
- 1 teaspoon (4 grams) vanilla extract
- 2 large eggs (100 grams), lightly beaten
- 2 cups (250 grams) all-purpose flour
- 2 teaspoons (10 grams) baking powder
- 2 teaspoons (10 grams) baking soda
- 1 teaspoon (3 grams) kosher salt
- Peanut Butter Frosting (recipe follows)
- Garnish: chopped chocolate

1. Preheat oven to 350°F (180°C). Line a 13x9-inch baking pan with parchment paper, letting parchment extend over sides of pan. Spray parchment with baking spray with flour.
2. In a large bowl, place chocolate and butter.
3. In a medium saucepan, bring 1½ cups (360 grams) water and sugars to a boil over medium-high heat, whisking occasionally until sugars dissolve. Remove from heat; whisk in cocoa until smooth.
4. Pour sugar mixture onto chocolate mixture; let stand for 2 minutes. Whisk until chocolate is melted and mixture is smooth. Whisk in sour cream and vanilla. Whisk in eggs until well combined.
5. In a medium bowl, whisk together flour, baking powder, baking soda, and salt. Slowly add flour mixture to chocolate mixture, whisking just until combined. Spread batter into prepared pan.
6. Bake until a wooden pick inserted in center comes out clean, 30 to 35 minutes. Let cool completely on a wire rack.
7. Spread Peanut Butter Frosting onto cake; garnish with chocolate, if desired. Store in an airtight container for up to 3 days.

Peanut Butter Frosting

Makes about 5 cups

- 1 cup (227 grams) unsalted butter, softened
- 1 cup (225 grams) cream cheese, softened
- 1½ cups (384 grams) creamy peanut butter
- 1 tablespoon (13 grams) vanilla extract
- 2 cups (240 grams) confectioners' sugar
- 2 tablespoons (30 grams) whole milk

1. In the bowl of a stand mixer fitted with the paddle attachment, beat butter and cream cheese at low speed until smooth. Add peanut butter and vanilla, beating until combined. Gradually add confectioners' sugar alternately with milk, beating until smooth. Increase mixer speed to medium, and beat until fluffy, 1 to 2 minutes. Use immediately.

MARBLE SHEET CAKE

Makes 1 (13x9-inch) cake

Swirls of rich chocolate-almond batter and sweet vanilla batter combine to create this stunning sheet cake. Top with a dusting of confectioners' sugar for a simple yet elegant finish.

- 3 cups (375 grams) all-purpose flour
- 1¾ cups (350 grams) granulated sugar
- 1 tablespoon (15 grams) baking powder
- 1 teaspoon (3 grams) kosher salt
- 1½ cups (360 grams) whole milk, room temperature
- ¾ cup (170 grams) plus 2 tablespoons (28 grams) unsalted butter, melted and divided
- 2 teaspoons (8 grams) vanilla extract
- 3 large eggs (150 grams), room temperature
- ⅓ cup (25 grams) unsweetened cocoa powder, sifted
- ½ teaspoon (2 grams) almond extract
- 2 tablespoons (14 grams) confectioners' sugar

1. Preheat oven to 325°F (170°C). Spray a 13x9-inch baking pan with baking spray with flour.
2. In the bowl of a stand mixer fitted with the paddle attachment, whisk together flour, granulated sugar, baking powder, and salt by hand; make a well in center. With mixer on low speed, add milk, ¾ cup (170 grams) melted butter, and vanilla, beating until almost smooth and stopping to scrape sides of bowl. Add eggs, one at a time, beating well after each addition. Spread 4¾ cups (about 1,000 grams) vanilla batter into prepared pan.
3. Add cocoa, almond extract, and remaining 2 tablespoons (28 grams) melted butter to remaining vanilla batter; whisk until smooth. Drop heaping tablespoonfuls of chocolate batter onto vanilla batter; swirl with the tip of a knife. Tap pan on counter twice to release air bubbles.
4. Bake until a wooden pick inserted in center comes out clean, about 35 minutes. Let cool completely on a wire rack.
5. Just before serving, sift confectioners' sugar onto cake. Store in an airtight container for up to 4 days.

pro tip

To swirl batter, slowly pull the tip of a knife from side to side, up and down, and diagonally through the batter.

MINI PINEAPPLE UPSIDE-DOWN CAKES

Makes 12 (2-inch) cakes

In this miniature take on the classic American dessert, the pineapple rings caramelizes while baking, creating the perfect topping for the tender cake. Buy and core a fresh pineapple yourself instead of buying precut and cored. This way, you control the amount of pineapple you take out when coring it.

- ¼ cup (57 grams) unsalted butter, melted
- ¾ cup (167 grams) firmly packed light brown sugar
- 1 fresh pineapple (about 905 grams), peeled, cored, and sliced into ¼-inch-thick rings
- 6 maraschino cherries (42 grams), drained and halved
- ½ cup (113 grams) unsalted butter, softened
- 1 cup (200 grams) granulated sugar
- 2 large eggs (100 grams), room temperature
- 1 tablespoon (18 grams) vanilla bean paste
- 1½ cups (188 grams) all-purpose flour
- 1½ teaspoons (7.5 grams) baking powder
- ½ teaspoon (1.5 grams) kosher salt
- ½ cup (120 grams) whole milk

1. Preheat oven to 350°F (180°C). Spray a 12-cup muffin pan (see Note) with baking spray with flour.
2. Fill each prepared muffin cup with 1 teaspoon (5 grams) melted butter. Add 1 tablespoon (14 grams) brown sugar to each cup, lightly pressing to form an even layer.
3. Using a round cutter the same diameter as the bottom of your muffin cups, cut mini pineapple rings, being careful to center cutter around cored hole. (I used a 2-inch cutter.) Place pineapple rings and cherries, cut side up, in muffin cups.
4. In the bowl of a stand mixer fitted with the paddle attachment, beat softened butter and granulated sugar at medium speed until fluffy, 3 to 4 minutes, stopping to scrape sides of bowl. Add eggs, one at a time, beating well after each addition. Beat in vanilla bean paste.
5. In a medium bowl, whisk together flour, baking powder, and salt. With mixer on low speed, gradually add flour mixture to butter mixture alternately with milk, beginning and ending with flour mixture, beating just until combined after each addition. Spoon batter (about 3 tablespoons) into each cup.
6. Bake until a wooden pick inserted in center comes out clean, 15 to 20 minutes. Let cool in pan for 10 minutes. Carefully invert cakes onto a baking sheet. Best served warn same day as made.

Note: *These look best in a muffin pan with straight-sided cups rather than sloped sides.*

BREADS

Baking bread, even yeasted bread, doesn't have to be an hours-long endeavour. These loaves, scones, biscuits, muffins, and more will show you how.

ENGLISH MUFFIN LOAF

Makes 1 (8½x4½-inch) loaf

Featuring a lightly crisp exterior and an airy, chewy interior, this loaf is everything you love about English muffins. Top toasted slices with butter and jam for breakfast, or layer on ingredients for your best-ever sandwich.

Cornmeal or semolina flour, for sprinkling
2½ cups (318 grams) bread flour
1 tablespoon (12 grams) granulated sugar
2½ teaspoons (7.5 grams) kosher salt
1 (0.25-ounce) package (7 grams) instant yeast*
¼ teaspoon (1.25 grams) baking soda
⅔ cup (160 grams) water
½ cup (120 grams) warm milk (120°F/49°C to 130°F/54°C)
2 tablespoons (28 grams) vegetable oil

1. Lightly spray an 8½x4½-inch loaf pan with baking spray with flour; sprinkle with cornmeal or semolina flour.
2. In a large bowl, whisk together bread flour, sugar, salt, yeast, and baking soda.
3. In a small bowl, whisk together ⅔ cup (160 grams) water, warm milk, and oil. Add milk mixture to flour mixture, stirring just until combined. Cover and let stand at room temperature for 15 minutes.
4. Preheat oven to 400°F (200°C).
5. Using a rubber spatula, fold dough onto itself a few times until dough is more elastic. Spread dough into prepared pan, and flatten top with wet fingertips. Sprinkle cornmeal or semolina flour onto dough. Cover and let rise in a warm, draft-free place (75°F/24°C) until doubled in size and dough almost fills pan, 25 to 30 minutes.
6. Bake until golden brown and an instant-read thermometer inserted in center registers 190°F (88°C), 20 to 25 minutes, covering with foil during final 5 minutes of baking to prevent excess browning. Let cool in pan for 15 minutes. Remove from pan, and let cool completely on a wire rack. Store in an airtight container for up to 3 days.

**I used Platinum® Yeast from Red Star®.*

pro tip

For an even more flavorful loaf, cover and refrigerate your dough overnight at the end of step 5. Let it come to room temperature and then let stand while your oven preheats.

APPLE-CHEDDAR-SAGE BISCUITS

Makes 12 biscuits

The golden-brown exterior of these biscuits gives way to a soft and tender interior that readily soaks up a generous slather of butter.

3¾ cups (469 grams) all-purpose flour, plus more for dusting
3½ teaspoons (14 grams) granulated sugar
1 tablespoon (15 grams) baking powder
1 tablespoon (9 grams) kosher salt
1 tablespoon (4 grams) packed fresh sage leaves, finely chopped
½ teaspoon (1 gram) ground black pepper
1 cup (227 grams) cold unsalted butter, cubed
1 cup (113 grams) shredded sharp Cheddar cheese
1 medium Gala or Honeycrisp apple (200 grams), peeled and shredded (see Notes)
¾ cup (180 grams) cold whole buttermilk
1 large egg (50 grams), lightly beaten
1 tablespoon (15 grams) water
Fresh sage leaves and flaked sea salt (optional)
Softened butter, to serve

1. Preheat oven to 425°F (220°C). Line a baking sheet with parchment paper.
2. In a large bowl, whisk together flour, sugar, baking powder, kosher salt, chopped sage, and pepper. Add cold butter, tossing to coat. Using a pastry blender or your hands, cut in butter until mixture is crumbly and butter pieces are pea-size. Stir in cheese and apple. Add cold buttermilk, and fold until a shaggy dough forms.
3. Turn out dough onto a lightly floured surface. (Dough will be crumbly and almost dry.) Pat dough into a rectangle about 1 inch thick. Using a lightly floured rolling pin, roll dough into about a 15x6-inch rectangle. Using a bench or bowl scraper, fold dough in thirds like a letter. Rotate dough 90 degrees. Repeat rolling, folding, and rotating 3 more times. (Dough will seem too shaggy to do this to start but will be easier to work with as you go.)
4. Pat or roll dough into a 9½x7½-inch rectangle (about 1 inch thick). Using a sharp knife or a floured bench scraper, trim ¼ inch off all sides, if desired. (See Notes.) Cut dough into 12 biscuits. Place 2 inches apart on prepared pan. Freeze until firm, about 10 minutes.
5. In a small bowl, whisk together egg and 1 tablespoon (15 grams) water; brush onto biscuits. Top with sage leaves (if using), and sprinkle with sea salt (if using).
6. Bake until golden brown, 15 to 20 minutes. Serve warm with butter.

Notes: *Peel the apple and shred it on a box grater just before adding it to the flour mixture.*

Trimming the edges of the dough helps the biscuits rise evenly, but this step is entirely optional. They'll taste great regardless.

MEXICAN STREET CORN BREAD WITH LIME BUTTER

Makes 1 (8½x4½-inch) loaf

Each slice of this moist bread is studded with fresh cilantro, buttery corn, and salty cheese—a generous slather of Lime Butter is a must!

- 1 cup (150 grams) finely ground plain yellow cornmeal
- ⅓ cup (42 grams) all-purpose flour
- 2 tablespoons (24 grams) granulated sugar
- 1½ teaspoons (7.5 grams) baking powder
- 1½ teaspoons (3 grams) chili powder
- 1 teaspoon (3 grams) kosher salt
- ½ teaspoon (2.5 grams) baking soda
- ½ teaspoon (1 gram) ground cumin
- ¾ cup (180 grams) full-fat sour cream, room temperature
- ½ cup (112 grams) vegetable oil
- ¼ cup (60 grams) whole milk, room temperature
- 2 large eggs (100 grams), room temperature
- 1 cup (141 grams) fresh or drained thawed frozen corn kernels, roasted (see Note)
- ½ cup (72 grams) crumbled queso fresco
- 3 tablespoons (6 grams) chopped fresh cilantro
- 2 teaspoons (6 grams) minced garlic (about 2 cloves)
- Lime Butter (recipe follows)

1. Preheat oven to 350°F (180°C). Spray an 8½x4½-inch loaf pan with baking spray with flour. Line pan with parchment paper, letting excess extend over sides of pan.
2. In a medium bowl, whisk together cornmeal, flour, sugar, baking powder, chili powder, salt, baking soda, and cumin.
3. In a large bowl, whisk together sour cream, oil, milk, and eggs. Add cornmeal mixture, and whisk until almost combined. Stir in corn, queso fresco, cilantro, and garlic until well combined. Spread batter into prepared pan.
4. Bake until golden brown and a wooden pick inserted in center comes out with a few moist crumbs, 40 to 50 minutes, covering with foil during final 10 minutes of baking to prevent excess browning. Let cool in pan on a wire rack for 10 minutes. Using excess parchment as handles, remove from pan; serve warm with Lime Butter. Store in an airtight container for up to 3 days.

Note: *To roast corn, heat 1 tablespoon (14 grams) olive oil in a large skillet over medium-high heat. Add corn; cook, stirring frequently, until golden brown, 4 to 5 minutes. Let cool before using.*

Lime Butter

Makes about ½ cup

- ½ cup (113 grams) unsalted butter, room temperature
- 2 teaspoons (2 grams) lime zest
- 1 teaspoon (2 grams) chili powder
- ½ teaspoon (1.5 grams) kosher salt

1. In a small bowl, stir together all ingredients until well combined. Refrigerate in an airtight container for up to 1 month.

CHÈVRE AND HERB QUICK BREAD

Makes 1 (8½x4½-inch) loaf

Flecked with basil, parsley, and chives and coming together in four simple steps, this aromatic bread will become your favorite savory loaf,

---

2½ cups (313 grams) all-purpose flour
1 tablespoon (12 grams) granulated sugar
1½ teaspoons (7.5 grams) baking powder
1½ teaspoons (4.5 grams) kosher salt
½ teaspoon (1 gram) ground black pepper
¼ teaspoon (1.25 grams) baking soda
1⅓ cups (320 grams) whole buttermilk, room temperature
¼ cup (56 grams) olive oil
1 large egg (50 grams), room temperature
¾ cup (170 grams) chèvre (goat cheese), crumbled
½ cup (12 grams) fresh basil leaves, finely chopped
½ cup (12 grams) fresh parsley leaves, finely chopped
⅓ cup (8 grams) finely chopped fresh chives

1. Preheat oven to 350°F (180°C). Spray an 8½x4½-inch loaf pan with baking spray with flour. Line pan with parchment paper, letting excess extend over sides of pan.
2. In a medium bowl, whisk together flour, sugar, baking powder, salt, pepper, and baking soda.
3. In a large bowl, whisk together buttermilk, oil, and egg. Add cheese and herbs. Fold in flour mixture until just combined. (Do not overmix.) Spread batter into prepared pan.
4. Bake until a wooden pick inserted in center comes out clean and an instant-read thermometer inserted in center registers 200°F (93°C), 55 minutes to 1 hour. Let cool in pan on a wire rack for 10 minutes. Using excess parchment as handles, remove from pan, and let cool completely on a wire rack. Store in an airtight container for up to 3 days.

GLUTEN-FREE TOMATO AND LEEK FOCACCIA

Makes 1 (13x9-inch) loaf

Focaccia is a perfect vehicle for most any topping you like, but I stuck to classic flavors with this gluten-free version. However, don't let that aspect deter you from making it. This bread bakes up just as airy, chewy, and pillowy as the original.

1½ cups (360 grams) warm water (105°F/41°C to 110°F/43°C)
4 teaspoons (16 grams) granulated sugar, divided
1 (0.25-ounce) package (7 grams) active dry yeast*
3⅓ cups (465 grams) gluten-free all-purpose flour (see Notes)
2 tablespoons (11 grams) dry milk (see Notes)
4 teaspoons (12 grams) kosher salt
1 tablespoon (9 grams) xanthan gum (see Notes)
1¼ teaspoons (6.25 grams) baking powder
¼ cup (57 grams) plus 2 tablespoons (28 grams) olive oil, divided
1 cup (140 grams) cherry or grape tomatoes, halved
1 tablespoon (3 grams) minced fresh oregano
¼ teaspoon ground black pepper
3 tablespoons (15 grams) sliced leek (white and light green parts only)
Garnish: flaked sea salt, chopped fresh oregano

1. In a small bowl, combine 1½ cups (360 grams) warm water, 1 teaspoon (4 grams) sugar, and yeast. Let stand until foamy, 5 to 10 minutes.
2. In the bowl of a stand mixer fitted with the paddle attachment, beat flour, dry milk, kosher salt, xanthan gum, baking powder, and remaining 3 teaspoons (12 grams) sugar at low speed just until combined. Add yeast mixture and ¼ cup (57 grams) oil. Beat at medium speed until combined and elastic, about 5 minutes. (Dough will be soft and sticky, almost resembling a thick muffin batter, but should hold together in a ball when you scrape the sides of the bowl.) Cover and let stand at room temperature for 30 minutes. (Dough will not fully rise but should puff.)
3. Generously spray a 13x9-inch baking pan with cooking spray. Line pan with parchment paper; spray parchment. Transfer dough to prepared pan. Using wet hands, carefully spread and press dough toward edges of pan in an even layer. Using your fingers, dimple surface. Cover and let stand for 30 minutes.
4. Position oven rack in center of oven. Preheat oven to 400°F (200°C).
5. Drizzle remaining 2 tablespoons (28 grams) oil onto dough. Top with tomatoes, oregano, and pepper. Place pan in oven.
6. Immediately reduce oven temperature to 375°F (190°C). Bake until top is puffed, about 20 minutes. Sprinkle leek on top. Bake until bread is golden brown, about 10 minutes more. Let cool in pan for 10 minutes. Remove from pan, and let cool on a wire rack for 20 minutes. Serve warm. Store in an airtight container for up to 3 days.

**I used Red Star® All-Natural Active Dry Yeast.*

Notes: *There are many varieties and blends of gluten-free flours; gluten-free all-purpose flour is different from a gluten-free cup-for-cup substitution, which does not work well for yeasted products. Be sure to use gluten-free all-purpose flour for this recipe.*

Adding dry milk to a gluten-free dough increases the protein content of the dough without impacting moisture level and doesn't add a noticeable flavor.

Xanthan gum is added to help bind and stabilize the dough.

SEEDED LAVASH

Makes 2 flatbreads

An aromatic blend of spices adds a level of complexity to this crisp Middle Eastern-inspired flatbread.

- **1½ cups (188 grams) all-purpose flour, plus more for dusting**
- **1½ teaspoons (4.5 grams) kosher salt, divided**
- **½ teaspoon (1.5 grams) instant yeast**
- **½ cup (120 grams) warm water (120°F/49°C to 130°F/54°C)**
- **4 tablespoons (56 grams) olive oil, divided**
- **2 teaspoons (4 grams) za'atar**
- **1 teaspoon (2 grams) sesame seeds**
- **1 teaspoon (2 grams) dried thyme**
- **Neutral oil, for brushing**

1. In a large bowl, whisk together flour, 1 teaspoon (3 grams) salt, and yeast. Add ½ cup (120 grams) warm water and 2 tablespoons (28 grams) olive oil; stir just until combined and no dry spots remain.

2. Turn out dough onto a lightly floured surface, and knead until dough is soft and elastic, about 5 minutes. (Dough will start out very sticky; use a bench scraper if needed. Do not add too much flour; the dough will come together.) Return dough to bowl, cover, and let stand for 30 minutes.

3. Preheat oven to 375°F (190°C). Brush 2 rimless baking sheets or bottom of 2 rimmed baking sheets with neutral oil.

4. In a small bowl, stir together za'atar, sesame seeds, dried thyme, and remaining ½ teaspoon (1.5 grams) salt.

5. Divide dough in half. On one prepared pan, carefully stretch half of dough into an 11½x9-inch rectangle. Brush 1 tablespoon (14 grams) olive oil onto dough. Sprinkle with half of za'atar mixture. Repeat with remaining dough, remaining 1 tablespoon (14 grams) olive oil, and remaining za'atar mixture.

6. Bake until golden brown and crisp, 20 to 25 minutes, rotating pans halfway through baking. Let cool completely on pans on a wire rack. Break into pieces to serve. Store in an airtight container for up to 5 days.

KEY LIME DOUGHNUTS

Makes 12 doughnuts

Key lime pie gets an irresistible makeover with these baked doughnuts. Lightly crisp on the outside and airy on the inside, these treats bring a bright pop of color to your day and a sweet tang to your mouth.

1¼ cups (156 grams) unbleached cake flour
¾ teaspoon (2.25 grams) kosher salt
½ teaspoon (2.5 grams) baking powder
¼ teaspoon (1.25 grams) baking soda
½ cup (100 grams) granulated sugar
2 tablespoons (6 grams) lime zest
¼ cup (60 grams) whole buttermilk, room temperature
1 large egg (50 grams), room temperature
5 tablespoons (75 grams) fresh or bottled Key lime juice, divided
3 tablespoons (42 grams) vegetable oil
1½ cups (180 grams) confectioners' sugar
Green and yellow liquid food coloring
Garnish: graham cracker crumbs, lime zest

1. Preheat oven to 400°F (200°C). Butter and flour 2 (6-well) doughnut pans.
2. In a small bowl, whisk together flour, salt, baking powder, and baking soda.
3. In a medium bowl, whisk together granulated sugar and lime zest until well combined. Whisk in buttermilk, egg, 3 tablespoons (45 grams) lime juice, and oil until combined. Add flour mixture, and whisk until just combined, stopping to scrape sides of bowl.
4. Transfer batter to a pastry bag, and cut a ½-inch opening in tip. Pipe batter into prepared wells (about 2 heaping tablespoons or 35 grams each).
5. Bake until puffed and edges are golden brown, 8 to 10 minutes, rotating pans halfway through baking. Let cool in pans for 10 minutes. Turn out doughnuts onto a wire rack, and let cool completely.
6. In a small bowl, whisk together confectioners' sugar and remaining 2 tablespoons (30 grams) lime juice. Tint with food coloring as desired. Carefully dip top of each doughnut into glaze. Garnish with graham cracker crumbs and lime zest, if desired. Store in an airtight container for up to 3 days.

pro tip

Zesting and juicing fresh Key limes can be difficult due to their small size, but if you like the challenge, go for it! For a shortcut, I've found that store-bought bottled Nellie & Joe's Famous Key West Lime Juice works just as well, as do regular limes.

JUMBO BLUEBERRY CORNMEAL MUFFINS

Makes 6 jumbo or 12 regular muffins

Say hello to your new favorite blueberry muffins, courtesy of my friend Jessie Sheehan. These not-too-sweet cuties are jam-packed with blueberries and have a subtle crunchy texture from the cornmeal. If you don't have a jumbo muffin pan, line 12 regular muffin cups with paper liners, divide the batter among the cups, and bake for 20 to 25 minutes.

---

1 cup (200 grams) granulated sugar
⅓ cup (75 grams) vegetable oil
2 teaspoons (8 grams) vanilla extract
2 large eggs (100 grams)
½ cup (120 grams) sour cream
1½ teaspoons (7.5 grams) baking powder
¼ teaspoon (1.25 grams) baking soda
½ teaspoon (1.5 grams) kosher salt
2 cups (280 grams) fresh or frozen blueberries
1½ cups (188 grams) all-purpose flour
½ cup (75 grams) plain cornmeal
Turbinado sugar, for sprinkling

1. Preheat oven to 400°F (200°C). Generously spray a 6-cup jumbo muffin pan with cooking spray.
2. In a large bowl, whisk together granulated sugar, oil, and vanilla for 30 seconds. Add eggs, one at a time, whisking until combined after each addition; whisk in sour cream. Sprinkle baking powder on top; whisk vigorously until combined. Repeat procedure with baking soda and then salt. Gently fold in 1½ cups (210 grams) blueberries, flour, and cornmeal just until no streaks of flour remain. Divide batter among prepared cups; press remaining ½ cup (70 grams) blueberries into top of batter. Generously sprinkle turbinado sugar on top.
3. Bake until a wooden pick inserted in center comes out with a few moist crumbs, 25 to 30 minutes, covering with foil during final 5 to 10 minutes of baking to prevent excess browning. Let cool in pan on a wire rack for 10 minutes. Serve warm.

SPICED APPLE SCONES

Makes 8 scones

Fragrant and not too sweet, these scones are best paired with a cup of coffee or tea for an afternoon snack.

- 2 cups (250 grams) all-purpose flour, plus more for dusting
- ¼ cup (50 grams) granulated sugar
- 2½ teaspoons (12.5 grams) baking powder
- 1½ teaspoons (2.5 grams) Chinese five-spice powder, divided
- 1 teaspoon (3 grams) kosher salt
- ¼ teaspoon (1.25 grams) baking soda
- 6 tablespoons (84 grams) cold unsalted butter, cubed
- 1 cup (120 grams) finely diced firm sweet apple
- 1 cup (240 grams) plus 8 tablespoons (120 grams) heavy whipping cream, divided
- 1½ teaspoons (9 grams) vanilla bean paste, divided
- 1 cup (120 grams) confectioners' sugar

1. Preheat oven to 375°F (190°C). Line a rimmed baking sheet with parchment paper.
2. In a large bowl, whisk together flour, granulated sugar, baking powder, 1¼ teaspoons (2.5 grams) five-spice powder, salt, and baking soda. Using a pastry blender or 2 forks, cut in cold butter until mixture resembles coarse crumbs. Stir in apple.
3. In a small bowl, stir together 1 cup (240 grams) cream and 1 teaspoon (6 grams) vanilla bean paste. Add cream mixture to flour mixture, and stir until combined and no dry streaks remain.
4. Turn out dough onto a lightly floured surface. Gently knead 2 to 3 times to bring dough together. Roll or pat dough into a 7-inch circle (about 1 inch thick). Using a floured knife or bench scraper, cut into 8 wedges. Place 2 inches apart on prepared pan. Freeze until firm, about 15 minutes.
5. Brush 2 tablespoons (30 grams) cream onto dough wedges.
6. Bake until golden brown and a wooden pick inserted in center comes out clean, 15 to 20 minutes. Let cool on pan for 10 minutes. Remove from pan, and let cool completely on a wire rack.
7. In a small bowl, whisk together confectioners' sugar, 5 tablespoons (75 grams) cream, remaining ½ teaspoon (3 grams) vanilla bean paste, and remaining ¼ teaspoon five-spice powder until smooth and pourable; whisk in up to remaining 1 tablespoon (15 grams) cream if needed. Drizzle glaze onto cooled scones. Store in an airtight container for up to 3 days.

CINNAMON-SUGAR POPOVERS WITH PEACH COMPOTE

Makes 6 popovers

For an easy treat with incredible bang for the buck, look no further than the always-delicious and gorgeous popover. This version from my friend Jessie Sheehan takes mere minutes to assemble, and they bake up tall and billowy in about 30 minutes. Popover pans make for a dramatically tall bake, but if you don't have one, fill the cups of a regular muffin pan two-thirds to three-fourths full and bake for about 30 minutes.

Popovers:

- 1⅓ **cups (320 grams) whole milk, room temperature**
- ¼ **cup (57 grams) unsalted butter, melted and cooled slightly**
- 4 **large eggs (200 grams), room temperature**
- 1 **teaspoon (4 grams) vanilla extract**
- 1⅓ **cups (167 grams) all-purpose flour**
- 1 **tablespoon (12 grams) granulated sugar**
- 1 **teaspoon (3 grams) kosher salt**

Topping:

- ½ **cup (100 grams) granulated sugar**
- 2 **teaspoons (4 grams) ground cinnamon**
- ¼ **cup (57 grams) unsalted butter, melted**

Peach Compote (recipe follows)

1. Preheat oven to 450°F (230°C). Place a 6-cup popover pan in oven to preheat.
2. For popovers: In a large bowl, whisk together milk, melted butter, eggs, and vanilla until frothy, about 1 minute. Whisk in flour, sugar, and salt until batter is slightly lumpy, about 30 seconds. (Do not whisk smooth.)
3. Carefully remove hot pan from oven, and spray with cooking spray. Divide batter among prepared cups.
4. Bake for 12 minutes. Rotate pan, and reduce oven temperature to 350°F (180°C). Bake until tall, golden brown, and crisp, 15 to 20 minutes more, covering with foil to prevent excess browning, if necessary.
5. Meanwhile, for topping: In a small bowl, whisk together sugar and cinnamon.
6. Carefully remove hot popovers from pan. Brush melted butter onto popovers, and generously sprinkle with cinnamon sugar to coat. Serve immediately with Peach Compote.

Peach Compote

Makes 1 cup

- 2 **cups (285 grams) diced fresh peaches (see Note)**
- 2 **tablespoons (24 grams) granulated sugar**
- 1 **tablespoon (15 grams) fresh lemon juice**
- ¼ **teaspoon kosher salt**
- ½ **teaspoon (2 grams) vanilla extract**

1. In a small saucepan, bring peaches, sugar, lemon juice, and salt to a boil over medium-high heat, stirring just until sugar dissolves. Reduce heat to medium; cook, stirring frequently, for 10 minutes. Remove from heat, and stir in vanilla. Let cool, stirring occasionally, before serving.

Note: *Peaches can be peeled or unpeeled for the compote, whichever is your preference.*

HUMMINGBIRD SCONES

Makes 4 scones

These Southern classic-inspired scones include every flavor of the beloved cake but in bread form. Filled with sweet banana, tangy pineapple, and crunchy pecans, these scones strike an ideal balance between decadence and light, fresh flavors.

1¾ cups (219 grams) all-purpose flour
3 tablespoons (36 grams) granulated sugar
½ teaspoon (2.5 grams) baking powder
1 teaspoon (2 grams) ground cinnamon
¾ teaspoon (2.25 grams) kosher salt
¼ teaspoon (1.25 grams) baking soda
6 tablespoons (84 grams) cold unsalted butter, cubed
¼ cup (60 grams) cold whole buttermilk
1 teaspoon (4 grams) vanilla extract
½ cup (114 grams) mashed ripe banana (about 1 medium banana)
¼ cup (67 grams) pressed drained crushed pineapple
½ cup (57 grams) chopped toasted pecans
Vanilla Cream Cheese Glaze (recipe follows)
Garnish: chopped toasted pecans

1. Preheat oven to 375°F (190°C). Line a baking sheet with parchment paper.
2. In a large bowl, whisk together flour, sugar, baking powder, cinnamon, salt, and baking soda. Using a pastry blender or your hands, cut in cold butter until it resembles course crumbs. Make a well in center.
3. In a medium bowl, whisk together cold buttermilk and vanilla. Add banana and pineapple. Add buttermilk mixture and pecans to flour mixture, and stir with a spatula until dry ingredients are fully moistened. Knead with your hands 1 or 2 times just until dough is smooth and fully hydrated.
4. Turn out dough, and pat into a 6-inch circle. Cut into 4 equal pieces. Place on prepared pan.
5. Bake until golden brown and an instant-read thermometer inserted in center registers 205°F (96°C), 25 to 30 minutes. Let cool on pan for 10 minutes. Remove from pan, and let cool completely on a wire rack.
6. Spread Vanilla Cream Cheese Glaze onto scones, and garnish with pecans, if desired. Store in an airtight container for up to 3 days.

Vanilla Cream Cheese Glaze

Makes about ¾ cup

4 ounces (113 grams) cream cheese, softened
¼ cup (30 grams) confectioners' sugar
2 tablespoons (30 grams) whole milk
1 teaspoon (4 grams) vanilla extract

1. In a small bowl, whisk together all ingredients until smooth.

PUMPKIN-CHOCOLATE SWIRL BREAD

Makes 1 (8½x4½-inch) loaf

This beautifully marbled quick bread loaf is as indulgent to eat as it is pretty to present.

1½ cups (188 grams) all-purpose flour
1 tablespoon (6 grams) pumpkin pie spice
2 teaspoons (10 grams) baking powder
1 teaspoon (3 grams) kosher salt
¼ teaspoon (1.25 grams) baking soda
1 cup (244 grams) canned pumpkin
½ cup (100 grams) granulated sugar
⅓ cup (73 grams) firmly packed light brown sugar
2 large eggs (100 grams), room temperature
3 tablespoons (42 grams) vegetable oil
1 teaspoon (4 grams) vanilla extract
½ cup (128 grams) hazelnut-chocolate spread*

1. Preheat oven to 350°F (180°C). Spray an 8½x4½-inch loaf pan with baking spray with flour. Line pan with parchment paper, letting excess extend over sides of pan.
2. In a medium bowl, whisk together flour, pie spice, baking powder, salt, and baking soda.
3. In a large bowl, whisk together pumpkin, sugars, eggs, oil, and vanilla until smooth. Whisk in flour mixture until thick and smooth. Spread half of batter (about 1¼ cups or 375 grams) into prepared pan.
4. Spoon hazelnut-chocolate spread into a pastry bag, and cut a ¼-inch opening in tip. Pipe half of spread evenly onto batter, leaving a ¼-inch border around edges. Using an offset spatula or skewer, gently swirl together spread and batter, avoiding sides of pan. Repeat procedure with remaining batter and remaining hazelnut-chocolate spread.
5. Bake until a wooden pick inserted in center comes out with a few moist crumbs, 50 to 55 minutes. Let cool in pan for 10 minutes. Using excess parchment as handles, remove from pan, and let cool completely on a wire rack. Store in an airtight container for up to 3 days.

**I used Bonne Maman® Hazelnut Chocolate Spread.*

Maman
Spread

BABÀ RUSTICO

Makes 1 (10-cup) loaf

A classic of Neapolitan cuisine, the babà rustico is a savory yeasted bread filled with Italian meats and cheeses and often baked in a ring mold.

2½ cups (318 grams) bread flour, divided
½ cup (48 grams) grated fresh Parmesan cheese
3 tablespoons (12 grams) chopped fresh parsley
2 teaspoons (6 grams) kosher salt
¼ teaspoon ground black pepper
1 cup (240 grams) warm whole milk (110°F/43°C to 115°F/46°C)
1 (0.25-ounce) package (7 grams) instant yeast*
1 teaspoon (4 grams) granulated sugar
4½ tablespoons (63 grams) neutral oil
2 large eggs (100 grams), room temperature
¾ cup (130 grams) ⅜-inch-cubed sharp provolone cheese
½ cup (80 grams) chopped salami Napoli
½ cup (90 grams) chopped prosciutto cotto
Garnish: chopped fresh parsley

1. In a medium bowl, whisk together 1½ cups (191 grams) flour, Parmesan, parsley, salt, and pepper.
2. In the bowl of a stand mixer, whisk together warm milk, yeast, and sugar by hand. Let stand until foamy, about 5 minutes. Add remaining 1 cup (127 grams) flour; using the paddle attachment, beat at low speed until smooth and well combined, about 1 minute. Add oil and eggs, and beat until well combined. With mixer on low speed, gradually add flour mixture, beating until well combined and stopping to scrape sides of bowl. Increase mixer speed to medium-high, and beat until dough is smooth, shiny, and elastic, 8 to 10 minutes. (Dough will still stick to sides and bottom of bowl.)
3. Reduce mixer speed to low, and gradually add provolone, salami, and prosciutto cotto until combined. (If you do not feel like the mix-ins are well distributed by the mixer, you can dip your hand in water, as needed, and fold and squeeze the dough to help distribute the mix-ins more evenly.) Cover and let stand at room temperature for 10 minutes.
4. Spray a 10-cup Bundt pan with baking spray with flour. Using a bowl scraper or spatula, spoon dough in small amounts evenly into prepared pan. Using wet fingers, evenly press dough into pan, even and flat. Tap pan on a kitchen towel-lined counter a few times. Cover and let rise in a warm, draft-free place (75°F/24°C) until dough is puffed and about 1 inch from top of pan, 30 to 45 minutes.
5. Preheat oven to 350°F (180°C).
6. Bake until golden and an instant-read thermometer inserted in center registers 190°F (88°C) to 200°F (93°C), 25 to 30 minutes. Let cool in pan for 5 minutes. Invert bread onto a wire rack, and let cool for 20 minutes. Serve warm. Cover and refrigerate for up to 3 days.

**I used Platinum® Yeast from Red Star®.*

DILL-SOUR CREAM-POTATO SCONES

Makes 10 scones

These scones boast an irresistibly fluffy texture thanks to mashed potatoes in the dough. Sour cream adds richness, and dill brings a tangy freshness.

---

3 cups (375 grams) all-purpose flour, plus more for dusting
2 tablespoons (8 grams) chopped fresh dill
4 teaspoons (20 grams) baking powder
2 teaspoons (8 grams) granulated sugar
1½ teaspoons (4.5 grams) kosher salt
½ teaspoon (1 gram) ground black pepper
½ cup (113 grams) cold unsalted butter, cubed
1 cup (232 grams) plain mashed russet potatoes, room temperature
⅔ cup (160 grams) cold sour cream
½ cup (120 grams) ice water
1 large egg (50 grams), lightly beaten
Sour cream, to serve

1. Preheat oven to 400°F (200°C). Line a baking sheet with parchment paper.
2. In a large bowl, whisk together flour, dill, baking powder, sugar, salt, and pepper. Using a pastry blender or 2 forks, cut in cold butter until mixture is crumbly.
3. In a small bowl, whisk together potatoes, cold sour cream, and ½ cup (120 grams) ice water. Add potato mixture to flour mixture, stirring with a fork just until mixture starts to come together. Using your hands, knead dough just until combined.
4. Turn out dough onto a lightly floured surface, and roll to 1-inch thickness. Using a 2½-inch round cutter dipped in flour, cut dough without twisting cutter, rerolling scraps once, and place at least 1 inch apart on prepared pan. Brush tops of scones with egg.
5. Bake until golden brown, 20 to 25 minutes. Let cool on pan for 5 minutes. Serve warm with sour cream.

HONEY-BUTTER YEAST ROLLS

Makes 16 rolls

These rolls are simple and light yet incredibly flavorful, with the perfect amount of buttery richness, honeyed sweetness, and gorgeous golden-brown color.

4½ to 4¾ cups (563 to 594 grams) all-purpose flour, divided, plus more for dusting
¼ cup (50 grams) granulated sugar
2¼ teaspoons (7 grams) instant yeast
1 teaspoon (3 grams) kosher salt
1 cup (240 grams) water
½ cup (120 grams) whole milk
½ cup (114 grams) unsalted butter, melted and divided
2 tablespoons (42 grams) honey
1 large egg (50 grams)

1. In the bowl of a stand mixer fitted with the paddle attachment, beat 2 cups (250 grams) flour, sugar, yeast, and salt at low speed just until combined.
2. In a small saucepan, heat 1 cup (240 grams) water, milk, ¼ cup (57 grams) melted butter, and honey over medium heat until an instant-read thermometer registers 120°F (49°C) to 130°F (54°C). Add warm milk mixture to flour mixture, and beat at low speed until combined, about 1 minute. Beat in egg until combined. Add 2½ cups (313 grams) flour, and beat until a shaggy dough forms, about 1 minute.
3. Switch to the dough hook attachment. Beat at low speed until dough is smooth, elastic, and slightly sticky, 10 to 12 minutes, stopping to scrape sides of bowl and dough hook; add up to remaining ¼ cup (31 grams) flour, 1 tablespoon (8 grams) at a time, if needed. Turn out dough onto a clean surface, and shape into a ball.
4. Lightly spray a large bowl with cooking spray. Place dough in bowl, turning to grease top. Cover and let rise in a warm, draft-free place (75°F/24°C) until doubled in size, 30 to 45 minutes.
5. Line 2 rimmed baking sheets with parchment paper.
6. On a lightly floured surface, roll dough into a 14x12-inch rectangle. Cut into 16 (3½x3-inch) rectangles, and place about ¼ inch apart on prepared pans. Cover and let rise in a warm, draft-free place (75°F/24°C) until puffed and dough holds an indentation when pressed, about 20 minutes.
7. Preheat oven to 375°F (190°C).
8. Bake until golden and an instant-read thermometer inserted in center registers 200°F (93°C), 12 to 15 minutes. Brush with remaining ¼ cup (57 grams) melted butter. Serve warm.

ROSEMARY-PARMESAN SODA BREAD

Makes 1 (8-inch) boule

The divine pairing of Parmesan and fresh rosemary strikes a perfect balance between the simple ingredients and deliciously complex flavors in this savory take on tradition.

- **4½ cups (563 grams) all-purpose flour, plus more for dusting**
- **2 tablespoons (24 grams) granulated sugar**
- **4 teaspoons (2.5 grams) chopped fresh rosemary**
- **2 teaspoons (6 grams) kosher salt**
- **1½ teaspoons (7.5 grams) baking soda**
- **¼ teaspoon ground black pepper**
- **1¼ cups (125 grams) grated fresh Parmesan cheese**
- **1¾ cups (420 grams) whole buttermilk**
- **¼ cup (57 grams) unsalted butter, melted**
- **1 large egg (50 grams)**
- **1½ teaspoons (4.5 grams) flaked sea salt**

1. Preheat oven to 425°F (220°C). Line a rimmed baking sheet with parchment paper.
2. In a large bowl, whisk together flour, sugar, rosemary, kosher salt, baking soda, and pepper. Stir in cheese.
3. In a medium bowl, whisk together buttermilk, melted butter, and egg. Gradually add buttermilk mixture to flour mixture, stirring just until dry ingredients are moistened. Knead dough just until ingredients are combined.
4. On a lightly floured surface, shape dough into a ball. Place on prepared pan, pressing to flatten dough into a 7-inch circle about 1½ inches thick. Using a sharp knife, score a shallow "X" on top of dough. Sprinkle with flaked salt.
5. Bake until golden brown and a wooden pick inserted in center comes out clean, 35 to 40 minutes, loosely covering with foil to prevent excess browning, if necessary. Let cool on pan for 20 minutes. Serve warm. Store in an airtight container for up to 3 days.

PUMPKIN SNICKERDOODLE MUFFINS

Makes 12 muffins

An inviting blend of warm snickerdoodle spice and delicately sweet pumpkin, these muffins offer a punched-up autumn flavor profile. Best of all, the stir-together batter can be whipped up in a flash and the streusel can be made ahead, giving you the perfect baked good when you need to make something delicious on the fly.

2½ cups (313 grams) all-purpose flour
1 cup (200 grams) granulated sugar, plus more for sprinkling
½ cup (110 grams) firmly packed light brown sugar
2¼ teaspoons (11.25 grams) baking powder
1½ teaspoons (3 grams) ground cinnamon
1 teaspoon (3 grams) kosher salt
½ teaspoon (1 gram) ground nutmeg
1 (15-ounce) can (425 grams) pumpkin
⅔ cup (149 grams) vegetable oil
½ cup (120 grams) whole milk, room temperature
3 large eggs (150 grams), room temperature
Snickerdoodle Streusel (recipe follows)

1. In a medium bowl, whisk together flour, sugars, baking powder, cinnamon, salt, and nutmeg.
2. In a large bowl, whisk together pumpkin, oil, milk, and eggs. Gradually add flour mixture, folding until combined and no flour pockets remain. (Batter will still be lumpy.) Cover with plastic wrap, and let stand at room temperature for 30 minutes.
3. Preheat oven to 375°F (190°C). Butter every other cup of 2 (12-cup) muffin pans. (See Note.) Sprinkle sides and bottoms of buttered cups with granulated sugar, tapping out any excess. (Alternatively, line muffin cups with paper liners.)
4. Spoon 7½ tablespoons (121 grams) batter into each prepared muffin cup. (Muffin cups will be extremely full, but batter will bake beautifully.) Sprinkle Snickerdoodle Streusel on top of batter (4 to 5 teaspoons or 15 grams each).
5. Bake for 10 minutes; reduce oven temperature to 350°F (180°C), and bake until a wooden pick inserted in center comes out clean, 12 to 15 minutes more. Let cool in pans for 15 minutes. Remove from pans, and let cool completely on a wire rack.

Note: *If you have only one 12-cup muffin pan, simply clean, cool, butter, and sugar pan between batches. Muffins can also be baked side by side in the same pan at the same time. Tops of muffins will touch when baking, but the end product will be just as delicious.*

Snickerdoodle Streusel

Makes 1¼ cups

½ cup (63 grams) all-purpose flour
⅓ cup (67 grams) granulated sugar
1¼ teaspoons (2.5 grams) ground cinnamon
½ teaspoon (1.5 grams) kosher salt
¼ cup (57 grams) cold unsalted butter, cut into ½-inch cubes

1. In a large bowl, stir together flour, sugar, cinnamon, and salt. Using a pastry blender or 2 forks, cut in cold butter until butter is pea-size or smaller. Pinch and rub pieces of butter into dry ingredients with fingertips until mixture comes together and resembles wet sand. Freeze for 20 minutes or until ready to use.

pro tip

Batter can be made the day before, covered, and refrigerated until ready to use.

CINNAMON CRUNCH BANANA BREAD

Makes 1 (8½x4½-inch) loaf

Just when you thought banana bread couldn't get any better, this moist, tender loaf takes all the comfort of the classic banana bread and adds a fun yet familiar twist of cinnamon sugar ribbons and a crunchy-sweet topping. This banana bread is bound to become a family favorite.

Filling:

2 tablespoons (16 grams) all-purpose flour
2 tablespoons (28 grams) firmly packed light brown sugar
2 teaspoons (4 grams) ground cinnamon
2 teaspoons (10 grams) unsalted butter, room temperature

Batter:

1⅔ cups (208 grams) all-purpose flour
¾ teaspoon (2.25 grams) kosher salt
½ teaspoon (2.5 grams) baking soda
¼ teaspoon (1.25 grams) baking powder
1 cup (240 grams) mashed ripe banana (about 3 medium bananas)
¾ cup (165 grams) firmly packed light brown sugar
¼ cup (56 grams) neutral oil
¼ cup (60 grams) sour cream, room temperature
2 large eggs (100 grams), room temperature
2 tablespoons (28 grams) unsalted butter, melted
1½ teaspoons (9 grams) vanilla bean paste

Cinnamon Sugar Topping (recipe follows)

1. Preheat oven to 325°F (170°C). Spray an 8½x4½-inch loaf pan with baking spray with flour. Line pan with parchment paper, letting excess extend over sides of pan.
2. For filling: In a small bowl, stir together flour, brown sugar, and cinnamon. Using your fingers, cut in butter until mixture is well combined and sandy.
3. For batter: In a medium bowl, whisk together flour, salt, baking soda, and baking powder.
4. In a large bowl, whisk together banana, brown sugar, oil, sour cream, eggs, melted butter, and vanilla bean paste. Gradually stir in flour mixture just until combined. Spread one-third of batter (about 1 cup or 280 grams) into prepared pan. Sprinkle with half of filling (about 2½ packed tablespoons or 30 grams), leaving a ⅛- to ¼-inch border around edges. Spread one-third of batter on top of filling in pan, and sprinkle with remaining filling, leaving a ⅛- to ¼-inch border around edges. Dollop remaining batter on top, and spread in an even layer. Sprinkle with Cinnamon Sugar Topping.
5. Bake for 40 minutes. Rotate pan, and bake until a wooden pick inserted in center comes out clean and an instant-read thermometer inserted in center registers 200°F (93°C) to 205°F (96°C), 26 to 32 minutes more, loosely covering with foil during final 10 to 12 minutes of baking to prevent excess browning. Let cool in pan on a wire rack for 10 minutes. Remove from pan, and let cool on wire rack for 10 minutes. Serve warm, or let cool completely.

Cinnamon Sugar Topping

Makes about 3 tablespoons

2 tablespoons (28 grams) firmly packed light brown sugar
1 teaspoon (3 grams) all-purpose flour
¼ teaspoon ground cinnamon
1 teaspoon (5 grams) cold unsalted butter

1. In a small bowl, stir together brown sugar, flour, and cinnamon. Using your fingers, cut in cold butter until mixture resembles coarse bread crumbs. Refrigerate until ready to use.

UPSIDE-DOWN HEIRLOOM TOMATO CORNBREAD

Makes 1 (10-inch) loaf

Loaded with fresh vegetables and cheese, this hearty, crispy-crusted cornbread is practically a meal itself.

- 3 medium heirloom tomatoes (369 grams), sliced into ½-inch-thick rounds and seeded (about 11 slices)
- 2 cups (240 grams) finely ground plain cornmeal
- 1 cup (125 grams) all-purpose flour
- 1 tablespoon (15 grams) baking powder
- 2 teaspoons (6 grams) kosher salt
- 2¼ cups (255 grams) shredded smoked white Cheddar cheese, divided
- 1 cup (154 grams) fresh corn kernels (about 2 ears corn)
- ½ cup (14 grams) finely sliced fresh basil
- ¼ cup (40 grams) minced seeded jalapeño
- 1¾ cups (420 grams) whole buttermilk
- 6 tablespoons (84 grams) unsalted butter, melted
- 2 large eggs (100 grams)
- 1 tablespoon (12 grams) granulated sugar

Garnish: fresh basil leaves

1. Preheat oven to 400°F (200°C). Line bottom of a 10-inch cast-iron skillet with parchment paper. Spray parchment and sides of skillet with cooking spray. Line a rimmed baking sheet with paper towels.
2. Place tomato slices on prepared baking sheet.
3. In a large bowl, whisk together cornmeal, flour, baking powder, and salt. Stir in 1½ cups (170 grams) cheese, corn, basil, and jalapeño.
4. In a medium bowl, whisk together buttermilk, melted butter, and eggs. Stir buttermilk mixture into cornmeal mixture just until combined.
5. In bottom of prepared skillet, place tomato slices, overlapping as needed. Sprinkle with sugar, and top with ½ cup (57 grams) cheese. Gently spread batter onto tomatoes.
6. Bake until golden brown and a wooden pick inserted in center comes out clean, 30 to 35 minutes, covering with foil to prevent excess browning, if necessary. Let cool in skillet for 10 minutes. Invert onto a serving plate.
7. Sprinkle with remaining ¼ cup (28 grams) cheese; garnish with basil, if desired. Serve hot.

pro tips

Any color of cornmeal will work in this recipe.

Lining the cast-iron skillet with parchment paper helps keep the acid in the tomatoes from wearing down the seasoning of your skillet. If you have an enamel-coated cast-iron skillet, you can skip this step.

Seeding the tomato slices and letting them drain on paper towels removes excess moisture that would otherwise make the cornbread soggy.

SUMMER HERB DINNER ROLLS

Makes 12 rolls

Your get-togethers deserve dinner rolls that rise to the occasion. These stunning knots have a prominent yeast flavor and a tall, pillowy crumb thanks to a generous helping of yeast in the dough. From the fresh herbs to a quick rise and an easy shaping method, this recipe is one you can customize to the seasons and enjoy all year long.

4¾ to 5 cups (594 to 625 grams) all-purpose flour, divided
¼ cup (50 grams) granulated sugar
4½ teaspoons (14 grams) instant yeast
1 tablespoon (9 grams) kosher salt
1 cup (240 grams) plus 1 tablespoon (15 grams) water, divided
½ cup (120 grams) sour cream
¼ cup (57 grams) plus 2 tablespoons (28 grams) unsalted butter, melted and divided
2 large eggs (100 grams), room temperature and divided
¼ cup (12 grams) finely chopped fresh chives
2 teaspoons (1.5 grams) finely chopped fresh dill
¼ teaspoon (1.5 grams) garlic salt

1. In the bowl of a stand mixer fitted with the paddle attachment, combine 1½ cups (188 grams) flour, sugar, yeast, and kosher salt.
2. In a medium saucepan, heat 1 cup (240 grams) water, sour cream, and ¼ cup (57 grams) melted butter over medium heat until an instant-read thermometer registers 120°F (49°C) to 130°F (54°C). Add warm sour cream mixture to flour mixture, and beat at medium speed until combined. Beat in 1 egg (50 grams) until combined. With mixer on low speed, gradually add 3¼ cups (406 grams) flour, chives, and dill, beating just until a shaggy dough forms.
3. Switch to the dough hook attachment. Beat at low speed until a soft, somewhat sticky dough forms, 7 to 8 minutes, stopping to scrape sides of bowl and dough hook. Add up to remaining ¼ cup (31 grams) flour, 1 tablespoon (8 grams) at a time, if dough is too sticky. Cover and let stand in a warm, draft-free place (75°F/24°C) for 10 minutes. (Dough will puff slightly.)
4. Line a 13x9-inch baking sheet with parchment paper.
5. Divide dough into 12 portions (about 93 grams each). With lightly floured hands, roll 1 portion into a 12-inch-long rope. (Keep remaining dough covered to prevent it from drying out.) Tie a loose knot toward one end of rope, leaving about 1 inch on one end. Pinch together both ends of dough under knot, forming a knotted ball. Place, seam side down, on prepared pan. Cover and let rise in a warm, draft-free place (75°F/24°C) until doubled in size, 20 to 30 minutes.
6. Preheat oven to 375°F (190°C).
7. In a small bowl, whisk together remaining 1 egg (50 grams) and remaining 1 tablespoon (15 grams) water. Brush tops of dough with egg wash.
8. Bake until golden brown and an instant-read thermometer inserted in center registers 190°F (88°C), 20 to 25 minutes, covering with foil to prevent excess browning, if necessary.
9. In a small bowl, stir together garlic salt and remaining 2 tablespoons (28 grams) melted butter; brush onto rolls. Serve warm.

FRESH CORN MUFFINS

Makes 10 to 12 muffins

These yeasted corn muffins are packed with prime summer produce, including fresh corn kernels, diced bell pepper, and bright dill. Alluringly savory yet sweet, these muffins will have you reaching for more.

- ⅓ cup (76 grams) plus 2 tablespoons (28 grams) unsalted butter, softened and divided
- ¾ cup (118 grams) fresh corn kernels
- ¾ cup (130 grams) minced red bell pepper
- 1 tablespoon (15 grams) minced garlic (3 to 4 cloves)
- 2 cups (250 grams) all-purpose flour, divided
- ½ cup (50 grams) finely ground yellow cornmeal
- ¼ cup (50 grams) granulated sugar
- 1 (0.25-ounce) package (7 grams) instant yeast*
- 2 teaspoons (6 grams) kosher salt
- 1 teaspoon (2 grams) onion powder
- ½ cup (120 grams) water
- ⅓ cup (80 grams) sour cream
- 1 large egg (50 grams), room temperature
- 2 tablespoons (5 grams) finely chopped fresh dill
- 1 tablespoon (14 grams) salted butter, melted

1. In a 12-inch skillet, melt 2 tablespoons (28 grams) unsalted butter over medium-high heat. Add corn, bell pepper, and garlic; cook, stirring frequently, until vegetables are tender, 4 to 6 minutes, adjusting heat as necessary to prevent excess browning. Remove from heat; let cool to room temperature.

2. In the bowl of a stand mixer fitted with the paddle attachment, beat 1 cup (125 grams) flour, cornmeal, sugar, yeast, salt, and onion powder at medium-low speed until combined.

3. In a medium saucepan, heat ½ cup (120 grams water, sour cream, and remaining ⅓ cup (76 grams) unsalted butter over medium heat until butter is melted and an instant-read thermometer registers 120°F (49°C) to 130°F (54°C). Add warm sour cream mixture to flour mixture; beat at medium-low speed until smooth and well combined, about 2 minutes, stopping to scrape sides of bowl. Add egg, dill, and remaining 1 cup (125 grams) flour; beat at low speed just until combined. Increase mixer speed to high, and beat for 2 minutes, stopping to scrape sides of bowl. (Mixture consistency will be a cross between a very thick cake batter and a very wet, slack dough.) Add cooled corn mixture; beat at low speed just until combined. Cover and let rise in a warm, draft-free place (75°F/24°C) until doubled in size, 40 minutes to 1 hour.

4. Spray a 12-cup muffin pan with cooking spray. Stir down batter, releasing as many air bubbles as possible. Divide batter among wells, filling up to ¼ inch from top rim (about 70 grams or a rounded ¼ cup each). (It's OK if not all wells get filled.) Using lightly greased fingertips, smooth tops of batter into an even layer. Cover with a greased sheet of plastic wrap, and let rise in a warm, draft-free place (75°F/24°C) until puffed, 20 to 25 minutes.

5. Preheat oven to 350°F (180°C).

6. Bake until golden brown, 20 to 23 minutes. Let cool in pan on a wire rack for 5 minutes. Remove from pan; brush with melted butter. Serve warm.

**I used Platinum® Yeast from Red Star®.*

VANILLA BEAN AND CARDAMOM SCONES

Makes 8 scones

A touch of warm cardamom and flecks of fragrant vanilla elegantly elevate the standard scone.

Scones:

- 2 cups (250 grams) all-purpose flour, plus more for dusting
- ¼ cup (50 grams) granulated sugar
- 1 tablespoon (15 grams) baking powder
- 2 teaspoons (6 grams) kosher salt
- ½ teaspoon (1 gram) ground cardamom
- 1 vanilla bean, split lengthwise, seeds scraped and reserved
- 5 tablespoons (70 grams) cold unsalted butter, cubed
- 1 cup (240 grams) plus 1 teaspoon (5 grams) heavy whipping cream, divided
- 1 large egg (50 grams)

Glaze:

- ¼ cup (50 grams) granulated sugar
- ¼ cup (60 grams) water
- 1 vanilla bean, split lengthwise, seeds scraped and reserved
- ½ cup (60 grams) confectioners' sugar

1. Preheat oven to 425°F (220°C). Lightly flour an 8-inch round cake pan. Line a baking sheet with parchment paper.

2. For scones: In the work bowl of a food processor, pulse flour, baking powder, granulated sugar, salt, cardamom, and reserved vanilla bean seeds. Add cold butter, and pulse until mixture is crumbly.

3. In a large bowl, stir together flour mixture and 1 cup (240 grams) cream just until combined. Turn out dough onto a lightly floured surface, and knead just until dough comes together. Press dough into prepared cake pan. Turn out dough; using a sharp knife or bench scraper cut into 8 wedges. Transfer wedges to prepared baking sheet.

4. In a small bowl, whisk together egg and remaining 1 teaspoon (5 grams) cream; brush onto dough.

5. Bake until golden brown, 12 to 15 minutes. Let cool on pan for 10 minutes.

6. For glaze: In a small saucepan, bring sugar, ¼ cup (60 grams) water, and reserved vanilla bean seeds and pod to a boil over medium heat, stirring until sugar dissolves. Reduce heat; simmer for 5 minutes.

7. Strain mixture through a fine-mesh sieve into a heatproof bowl, discarding solids.

8. In a small bowl, whisk together confectioners' sugar and 2 tablespoons vanilla syrup until smooth. Drizzle onto warm scones. Best served warm same day as made. Reseve remaining vanilla syrup for another use.

ANGEL BISCUITS

Makes about 11 biscuits

I love this combination of a traditional Southern biscuit and a Parker House roll. Their pillowy softness and golden buttery top will impress everyone at your table—and after the first bite, you'll never question its name again.

- ¼ cup (57 grams) cold all-vegetable shortening, cubed
- ¼ cup (57 grams) cold unsalted butter, cubed
- 2 tablespoons (28 grams) warm water (105°F/41°C to 110°F/43°C)
- 1 teaspoon (3 grams) active dry yeast
- 2 tablespoons (24 grams) granulated sugar
- 1½ cups (188 grams) all-purpose flour, plus more for dusting
- 1¼ cups (156 grams) cake flour
- 2 teaspoons (6 grams) kosher salt
- ½ teaspoon (2.5 grams) baking powder
- ¼ teaspoon (1.25 grams) baking soda
- 1 cup (240 grams) whole buttermilk
- 2 tablespoons (28 grams) salted butter, melted

1. Line a baking sheet with parchment paper.
2. Using a bench scraper, cut shortening and cold unsalted butter into cubes, and freeze until ready to use.
3. In a small bowl, stir together 2 tablespoons (30 grams) warm water and yeast until yeast dissolves. Stir in sugar; let stand until mixture is foamy, about 5 minutes.
4. In a large bowl, whisk together flours, salt, baking powder, and baking soda. Place three-fourths of flour mixture in the work bowl of a food processor; add cold shortening and cold butter, and pulse until mixture is crumbly with some pea-size pieces of butter remaining. (Alternatively, cut cold shortening and cold butter into flour mixture using a pastry blender.)
5. Return mixture to large bowl, and stir to combine with remaining flour mixture. Add yeast mixture and buttermilk, stirring just until dry ingredients are moistened. Cover and refrigerate for 1 hour.
6. Turn out dough onto a lightly floured surface, and knead 4 to 5 times. Pat dough to ¾-inch thickness. Using a 2½-inch round cutter, cut dough, re-patting scraps only once. Place on prepared pan. Cover and let rise in a warm, draft-free place (75°F/24°C) until puffed, about 1 hour.
7. Preheat oven to 375°F (190°C).
8. Brush with melted butter. Bake until golden brown, 12 to 15 minutes. Let cool on pan for 5 minutes. Serve warm.

PIES AND TARTS

Indulge in familiar sweet favorites and savory new flavors enveloped by buttery, flaky pastry and crunchy crumb crusts

HEIRLOOM TOMATO AND APRICOT TART

Makes 1 (9-inch) tart

With a buttery, nutty crust, a rich cheese-and-herb filling, and a sweet-savory topping, this tart brings seasonal treasures together.

---

1 cup (225 grams) ricotta cheese
4 large egg yolks (74 grams)
2 teaspoons (7 grams) minced garlic
1 teaspoon (3 grams) kosher salt
½ teaspoon (1 gram) ground black pepper
¾ cup (75 grams) shredded mozzarella cheese, divided
¼ cup (8 grams) chopped fresh basil
Pine Nut Crust (recipe follows)
2 heirloom tomatoes (638 grams), sliced ¼ inch thick and cut into thirds
6 fresh apricots (210 grams), sliced ¼ inch thick
Balsamic glaze and fresh basil leaves, to serve

1. Preheat oven to 350°F (180°C).
2. In a medium bowl, whisk together ricotta, egg yolks, garlic, salt, and pepper. Stir in ½ cup (50 grams) mozzarella and chopped basil. Spread mixture into cold prepared Pine Nut Crust.
3. Place tomato and apricot on ricotta mixture as desired. Sprinkle with remaining ¼ cup (25 grams) mozzarella.
4. Bake until filling is set, 45 to 60 minutes, covering with foil to prevent excess browning, if necessary. Let cool on a wire rack for 20 minutes. Remove tart from pan; transfer to a serving plate
5. Drizzle with balsamic glaze, and sprinkle with basil leaves. Serve warm. Refrigerate in an airtight container for up to 2 days.

Pine Nut Crust

Makes 1 (9-inch) crust

1 cup (96 grams) ground toasted pine nuts (see Note)
½ teaspoon (1.5 grams) kosher salt
½ teaspoon (1 gram) ground black pepper
1½ cups (188 grams) all-purpose flour
½ cup (113 grams) unsalted butter, softened
1 large egg yolk (19 grams)
1 teaspoon (5 grams) water

1. In the work bowl of a food processor, pulse pine nuts, salt, and pepper until combined. Add flour, and pulse until finely ground.
2. In the bowl of a stand mixer fitted with the paddle attachment, beat nut mixture, butter, egg yolk, and 1 teaspoon (5 grams) water at medium speed until combined. Wrap in plastic wrap, and refrigerate for 15 minutes.
3. Press dough into bottom and up sides of a 9-inch removable-bottom fluted tart pan. Freeze for 20 minutes.

Note: *To toast pine nuts, heat them in a small, dry skillet over medium heat, stirring frequently, until lightly browned and fragrant. Let cool before using.*

SPANAKOPITA

Makes 1 (9-inch) pie

A traditional Greek spinach pie, spanakopita is everything you want in a savory bake. Bright and herby, accented with lemon, and full of tangy feta cheese and spinach, this crisp phyllo pie can be served as a standalone dish or alongside a feast. Simple yet stunning, this Greek staple is a favorite for a reason.

---

3 tablespoons (42 grams) extra-virgin olive oil
½ yellow onion (87 grams), thinly sliced
2 cloves garlic (4 grams), minced
1 teaspoon (3 grams) kosher salt
½ teaspoon (1.5 grams) cracked black pepper
2 (10-ounce) packages frozen chopped spinach, thawed and drained
1½ cups (230 grams) crumbled feta cheese
⅓ cup (7 grams) chopped fresh basil
¼ cup (20 grams) shredded Parmesan cheese
¼ cup (7 grams) chopped fresh dill
2 large eggs (100 grams), room temperature
1 teaspoon (3 grams) lemon zest
15 sheets (about 188 grams) frozen phyllo pastry, thawed according to package directions
¾ cup (170 grams) unsalted butter, melted
Garnish: chopped fresh basil, chopped fresh dill

1. In a large skillet, heat oil over medium heat. Add onion, and cook, stirring occasionally, until beginning to soften, 1 to 2 minutes. Add garlic, salt, and pepper; cook, stirring occasionally, until fragrant and onions are translucent, 2 to 3 minutes. Transfer to a large bowl.
2. Add spinach to onion mixture, and stir until combined. Add feta, basil, Parmesan, dill, eggs, and lemon zest. Stir until combined.
3. Preheat oven to 350°F (180°C). Line a baking sheet with parchment paper.
4. Unfold phyllo pastry, and cover with parchment paper and a damp cloth to keep phyllo from drying out while you work. Place 1 sheet of phyllo on prepared pan, and brush with melted butter. Repeat with 2 sheets of phyllo, brushing each with melted butter. Place fourth sheet of phyllo perpendicular to previous, creating a "+" shape. Layer 2 more sheets of phyllo on top, brushing each with melted butter. Place seventh sheet of phyllo to create beginning of an "X" over the "+." Brush top with melted butter, and layer 2 more sheets of phyllo on top, brushing each with melted butter. Repeat with 3 more sheets to finish the "X" shape on the other side (12 sheets of phyllo total).
5. Spoon spinach mixture into center of phyllo sheets in pan; pat into an 8-inch circle. Fold excess phyllo over spinach mixture, using parchment to help lift phyllo as needed. Layer remaining 3 sheets of phyllo on top of pie to cover filling, brushing a layer of melted butter in between each. Drizzle any remaining melted butter on top.
6. Bake until phyllo is golden brown, about 45 minutes. Garnish with basil and dill, if desired. Let stand for 15 minutes; serve warm. Cover and refrigerate for up to 2 days.

HONEY PIE

Makes 1 (9-inch) pie

This dessert offers all the creamy sweetness of buttermilk pie but with heaps of floral honey flavor.

Crust:

1¾ cups (219 grams) all-purpose flour, plus more for dusting
1 tablespoon (12 grams) granulated sugar
1 teaspoon (3 grams) kosher salt
½ cup (113 grams) cold unsalted butter, cubed
2 tablespoons (30 grams) apple cider vinegar
4 to 5 tablespoons (60 to 75 grams) ice water
1 large egg (50 grams), lightly beaten

Filling:

¾ cup (255 grams) honey
¾ cup (180 grams) heavy whipping cream
½ cup (100 grams) granulated sugar
½ cup (113 grams) unsalted butter, melted
3 large eggs (150 grams)
1 tablespoon (9 grams) finely ground plain yellow cornmeal
1 tablespoon (15 grams) apple cider vinegar
1 teaspoon (4 teaspoons) vanilla extract
½ teaspoon (1.5 grams) kosher salt

1. For crust: In the work bowl of a food processor, pulse flour, sugar, and salt. Add butter, and pulse until mixture is crumbly. Add vinegar. Add water, 1 tablespoon (15 grams) at time, just until dough comes together. Turn out dough, and shape into a disk. Wrap tightly in plastic wrap, and refrigerate for 30 minutes.

2. On a lightly floured surface, roll dough to ¼-inch thickness. Transfer to a 9-inch pie plate, pressing into bottom and up sides. Trim excess dough to ¼ inch beyond edge of plate. (To create leaf decoration, roll dough scraps to ¼-inch thickness. Using a 1-inch leaf cutter, cut out leaf shapes. Brush edges of crust with egg wash, and gently press leaves onto crust.) Brush edges of crust with egg wash. Refrigerate for 15 minutes.

3. Position oven rack in bottom third of oven. Preheat oven to 350°F (180°C).

4. For filling: In a large bowl, whisk together honey, cream, sugar, melted butter, eggs, cornmeal, vinegar, vanilla, and salt. Pour into prepared crust.

5. Bake until center is set, about 45 minutes, covering with foil to prevent excess browning, if necessary. Let cool on a wire rack for 1 hour. Serve warm. Store in an airtight container for up to 3 days.

APRICOT FRANGIPANE TART

Makes 1 (14x4-inch) tart

I love the crunchy texture that almond flour gives this not-too-sweet crust. Smooth frangipane, an almond pastry cream, adds another nutty element and it's a great base for the fresh, juicy apricots in both taste and texture.

- **1¼ cups (120 grams) almond flour (see Note), divided**
- **1 cup (125 grams) all-purpose flour, plus more for dusting**
- **½ cup (100 grams) plus 1 teaspoon (4 grams) granulated sugar, divided**
- **½ teaspoon (1.5 grams) kosher salt**
- **7 tablespoons (98 grams) cold unsalted butter**
- **3 tablespoons (45 grams) cold water**
- **½ cup (113 grams) unsalted butter, softened**
- **2 large eggs (100 grams)**
- **1 teaspoon (5 grams) dark rum**
- **¼ teaspoon (1 gram) almond extract**
- **4 small apricots (250 grams), peeled and halved**
- **3 tablespoons (60 grams) apricot jam, warmed and strained**

1. In the work bowl of a food processor, pulse ¼ cup (24 grams) almond flour, all-purpose flour, 1 teaspoon (4 grams) sugar, and salt until combined. Add cold butter, and pulse until mixture is crumbly. With processor running, add 3 tablespoons (45 grams) cold water in a slow, steady stream just until dough comes together but is not sticky. (You may not need all the water.) Shape dough into a disk, and wrap in plastic wrap. Refrigerate for 30 minutes.
2. In the bowl of a stand mixer fitted with the paddle attachment, beat softened butter and remaining ½ cup (100 grams) sugar at medium-high speed until creamy, 3 to 4 minutes, stopping to scrape sides of bowl. Reduce mixer speed to low. Add eggs, one at a time, beating just until combined after each addition. Stir in rum and almond extract. Stir in remaining 1 cup (96 grams) almond flour just until combined.
3. Lightly spray a 14x4-inch fluted removable-bottom tart pan with baking spray with flour.
4. Lightly dust surface with all-purpose flour; on surface, roll dough into a 15x5-inch rectangle. Transfer to prepared pan, pressing into bottom and up sides. Trim edges of dough, and freeze in pan for 10 minutes.
5. Preheat oven to 350°F (180°C).
6. Top crust with a piece of parchment paper, letting ends extend over edges of pan; add pie weights.
7. Bake until edges are just set, 10 to 12 minutes. Carefully remove parchment and weights; bake for 2 minutes more. Let cool. Leave oven on.
8. Spread filling into cooled crust. Top with apricots, cut side down. Place tart pan on a rimmed baking sheet to catch any drips.
9. Bake until lightly browned, 40 to 45 minutes. Let cool on a wire rack for 20 minutes.
10. Remove from pan; brush jam onto apricots. Serve warm. Store in an airtight container for up to 3 days.

Note: *I recommend using almond flour made from blanched whole almonds; flour made with unblanched almonds will give your bakes a slightly grainier texture and darker color.*

CHOCOLATE-TOFFEE PECAN PIE

Makes 1 (9-inch) pie

If you're feeling fancy, this is the pie for you! Pecans are added to both the piecrust and the filling for a stronger toasted, nutty crunch, while a splash of bourbon enhances the rich notes of butter and vanilla and bits of toffee candy add a chocolate-caramel element that changes the game.

Pecan Piecrust (recipe follows)
1 cup (336 grams) light corn syrup
½ cup (100 grams) granulated sugar
½ cup (110 grams) firmly packed dark brown sugar
3 large eggs (150 grams), room temperature
2 tablespoons (28 grams) unsalted butter, melted and cooled
1 tablespoon (15 grams) bourbon
1 teaspoon (4 grams) vanilla extract
½ teaspoon (1.5 grams) kosher salt
1¾ cups (198 grams) pecan halves
½ cup (80 grams) finely chopped chocolate-covered toffee candy bar

1. Position oven racks in center and top third of oven. Preheat oven to 375°F (190°C). Spray a 9-inch pie plate with baking spray with flour.
2. On a lightly floured surface, roll Pecan Piecrust into a 12-inch circle (about ⅛ inch thick). Transfer to prepared plate, pressing into bottom and up sides; trim edges to ½ inch beyond edge of plate. Fold edges under, and crimp as desired. Freeze while preparing filling.
3. In a medium bowl, whisk together corn syrup, sugars, eggs, melted butter, bourbon, vanilla, and salt. Reserve ½ cup (57 grams) pecans; very roughly chop remaining 1¼ cups (141 grams) pecans. Fold all pecans and candy bar into corn syrup mixture. Pour into prepared crust.
4. Bake on center rack for 25 minutes. Place a sheet of foil on top rack, and bake until center of pie is set and an instant-read thermometer inserted in center registers 200°F (93°C), 40 to 45 minutes more, loosely covering with foil after 25 to 30 minutes of baking to prevent excess browning. Let cool completely on a wire rack before slicing.

Pecan Piecrust

Makes 1 (9-inch) crust

1½ cups (188 grams) all-purpose flour
½ cup (58 grams) pecan flour
1¼ teaspoons (3.75 grams) kosher salt
1 teaspoon (4 grams) granulated sugar
½ teaspoon (1 gram) ground cinnamon
¼ teaspoon ground nutmeg
½ cup (113 grams) cold unsalted butter, cubed
¼ cup (60 grams) ice water

1. In the work bowl of a food processor, pulse flours, salt, sugar, cinnamon, and nutmeg until combined. Add cold butter, and pulse until butter pieces are pea-size. With processor running, add ¼ cup (60 grams) ice water in a slow, steady stream just until dough starts to form large clumps. (Mixture should be moist and hold together when pinched.)
2. Turn out dough, and shape into a disk. Wrap tightly in plastic wrap, and refrigerate for 30 minutes.

PEAR AND HONEYED GOAT CHEESE GALETTE

Makes 1 (10-inch) galette

This buttery beauty is great for breakfast, brunch, or dessert. A sugared golden crust encircles warm, tangy goat cheese and sweet Bosc pears, which bake into a deep rustic hue. Thanks to the layered pears, the gorgeous design is effortless and accentuates the fruit's natural shape.

- 2 cups (250 grams) all-purpose flour, plus more for dusting
- 1 teaspoon (3 grams) kosher salt
- ¾ cup (170 grams) cold unsalted butter, cubed
- 4 ounces (115 grams) cold goat cheese
- 1 tablespoon (15 grams) apple cider vinegar
- 2 tablespoons (30 grams) ice water
- 6 ounces (175 grams) goat cheese, softened
- 3 tablespoons (63 grams) clover honey
- 1½ tablespoons (21 grams) firmly packed light brown sugar
- ¼ teaspoon ground nutmeg
- 3 slightly firm medium Bosc pears (537 grams)
- 1 large egg (50 grams)
- 1 tablespoon (15 grams) water
- 1 tablespoon (12 grams) granulated sugar

Garnish: clover honey, fresh rosemary

1. In the work bowl of a food processor, pulse flour and salt until combined. Add cold butter and cold goat cheese, and pulse until mixture is crumbly. Add vinegar, pulsing until combined. With processor running, add ice water, 1 tablespoon (15 grams) at a time, just until dough comes together.

2. Turn out dough, and shape into a disk. Wrap in plastic wrap, and refrigerate for 30 minutes.

3. In a medium bowl, whisk together softened goat cheese and honey until smooth. Whisk in brown sugar and nutmeg.

4. Preheat oven to 425°F (220°C). Line a baking sheet with parchment paper.

5. On a lightly floured surface, roll dough into a 14-inch circle (about ¼ inch thick). Transfer to prepared pan.

6. Cut pears in half vertically through stems. Scoop out core of each half. Place pears cut side down, and cut into thin slices, leaving about ½ inch intact below stem. Fan pears out, and place on filling, overlapping as needed. Fold edges of dough over pears.

7. In a small bowl, whisk together egg and 1 tablespoon (15 grams) water. Brush egg wash onto dough, and sprinkle with granulated sugar.

8. Bake until crust is golden brown and bottom is browned, 25 to 35 minutes. Let cool on pan for 10 minutes. Garnish with honey and rosemary, if desired. Serve warm or at room temperature.

STONE FRUIT GALETTE

Makes 1 (9-inch) galette

Buttery crust cradles jeweled nectarines, plums, and apricots that are minimally dressed so their fresh sweetness shines.

- **½ pound (226 grams) fresh apricots (about 2 small apricots), halved, pitted, and sliced ½ inch thick**
- **½ pound (226 grams) fresh plums (about 2 medium plums), halved, pitted, and sliced ½ inch thick**
- **½ pound (226 grams) fresh peaches (about 2 medium peaches), halved, pitted, and sliced ½ inch thick**
- **¼ cup (50 grams) granulated sugar**
- **2 teaspoons (6 grams) cornstarch**
- **1 teaspoon (3 grams) kosher salt**
- **1 teaspoon (1 gram) lemon zest**
- **¼ teaspoon grated fresh ginger**
- **All-purpose flour, for dusting**
- **All-Butter Pie Dough (recipe follows)**
- **1 large egg (50 grams)**
- **1 tablespoon (15 grams) water**
- **Turbinado sugar, for sprinkling**

1. Line a baking sheet with parchment paper.
2. In a large bowl, stir together all fruit, granulated sugar, cornstarch, salt, lemon zest, and ginger.
3. On a lightly floured surface, roll All-Butter Pie Dough into a 14-inch circle. Transfer to prepared pan. Using the back of a knife, lightly score a 9-inch circle in center of dough. Arrange fruit within circle as desired. Fold excess dough over fruit, pleating and folding as desired. Refrigerate until firm, about 20 minutes.
4. Preheat oven to 400°F (200°C).
5. In a small bowl, whisk together egg and 1 tablespoon (15 gram) water. Brush onto edges of dough. Sprinkle turbinado sugar onto dough and fruit. Transfer galette to oven.
6. Immediately reduce oven temperature to 375°F (190°C). Bake until fruit is soft and crust is golden brown, 40 to 50 minutes, covering with foil during final 10 minutes of baking to prevent excess browning. Let cool on pan on a wire rack for 10 minutes. Remove from pan, and let cool on a wire rack for 30 minutes; serve warm. Store in an airtight container for up to 3 days.

ALL-BUTTER PIE DOUGH

Makes 1 (9-inch) crust

- **1½ cups (188 grams) all-purpose flour**
- **1 teaspoon (3 grams) kosher salt**
- **½ cup (113 grams) cold unsalted butter, cubed**
- **⅓ cup (80 grams) ice water**

1. In the work bowl of a food processor, pulse flour and salt until combined. Add cold butter, and pulse until mixture is crumbly and butter is pea-size. With processor running, add ⅓ cup (80 grams) ice water in a slow, steady stream just until dough comes together. (Mixture may appear crumbly but should be moist and hold together when pinched.)
2. Turn out dough, and shape into a disk. Wrap in plastic wrap, and refrigerate for 1 hour.

pro tip

I like leaving the peel on the fruit for this galette—it brings beautiful color to the dessert and helps the fruit stay intact during baking.

PEACH, BLACKBERRY, AND BOURBON CROSTATA

Makes 1 (10-inch) crostata

The crostata, an Italian rustic tart, may seem an unlikely vessel for juicy peaches. But take one bite of this richly crusted treat, and you'll find a uniquely Southern combination of jammy peach and blackberry filling with a splash of warm bourbon.

---

4 cups (900 grams) sliced fresh peaches (about 5 medium peaches), peeled if desired
½ cup (110 grams) firmly packed light brown sugar
2 tablespoons (16 grams) all-purpose flour, plus more for dusting
2 tablespoons (16 grams) cornstarch
3 tablespoons (45 grams) bourbon, divided
⅛ teaspoon kosher salt
Crostata Dough (recipe follows)
½ cup (85 grams) fresh blackberries, sliced
1 large egg (50 grams)
1 teaspoon (5 grams) water
1 tablespoon (12 grams) turbinado sugar

1. Preheat oven to 375°F (190°C). Line a large rimmed baking sheet with parchment paper.
2. In a large bowl, stir together peaches, brown sugar, flour, cornstarch, 2 tablespoons (30 grams) bourbon, and salt.
3. On a lightly floured surface, roll Crostata Dough into a 12-inch circle. Transfer to prepared pan. Arrange peach mixture in center of Crostata Dough, leaving a 2-inch border around edges. Top with blackberries. Fold edges of dough over fruit, pleating crust as needed.
4. In a small bowl, whisk together egg and 1 teaspoon (5 grams) water; brush onto dough. Sprinkle with turbinado sugar.
5. Bake for 20 minutes. Cover filling with foil, and bake until crust is golden brown, about 25 minutes more. Let cool for 20 minutes. Brush filling with remaining 1 tablespoon (15 grams) bourbon. Serve warm. Store in an airtight container for up to 2 days.

CROSTATA DOUGH

Makes 1 (10-inch) crust

1¼ cups (156 grams) all-purpose flour
2 teaspoons (8 grams) granulated sugar
1 teaspoon (3 grams) kosher salt
½ cup plus 1 tablespoon (127 grams) cold unsalted butter, cubed
5 to 6 tablespoons (90 grams) ice water, divided

1. In the work bowl of a food processor, pulse flour, sugar, and salt until combined. Add cold butter; pulse until mixture is crumbly. With processor running, add 5 tablespoons (75 grams) ice water in a slow, steady stream just until dough comes together; add remaining 1 tablespoon (15 grams) ice water, if needed. Turn out dough, and shape into a disk. Wrap in plastic wrap, and refrigerate for 1 hour.

PEANUT BUTTER PIE

Makes 1 (9-inch) pie

Think of this as a giant, sophisticated take on a peanut butter cup. A decadent peanut butter mousse studded with roasted, salted peanuts tops a bittersweet ganache base and a chocolate cookie crust.

Crust:

1½ cups (184 grams) crushed chocolate wafer cookies
6 tablespoons (84 grams) unsalted butter, melted
¼ cup (50 grams) granulated sugar
⅛ teaspoon kosher salt

Ganache:

4 ounces (113 grams) bittersweet chocolate, finely chopped
¼ cup (60 grams) heavy whipping cream

Filling:

1 (8-ounce) package (226 grams) cream cheese, softened
1 cup (256 grams) creamy peanut butter
½ cup (57 grams) roasted salted peanuts, chopped
¼ cup (50 grams) granulated sugar
¼ cup (85 grams) honey
1 cup (240 grams) heavy whipping cream

1. Preheat oven to 350°F (180°C).
2. For crust: In a medium bowl, stir together crushed cookies, melted butter, sugar, and salt. Using a measuring cup, press mixture into bottom and up sides of a 9-inch pie plate.
3. Bake until set, about 10 minutes. Let cool.
4. For ganache: In a small microwave-safe bowl, heat chocolate and cream on high in 30-second intervals, stirring between each, until mixture is melted and smooth (about 1½ minutes total). Spread into cooled crust. Refrigerate until ganache is set, 15 to 20 minutes.
5. For filling: In the bowl of a stand mixer fitted with the paddle attachment, beat cream cheese and peanut butter at high speed until smooth. Add peanuts, sugar, and honey, beating until combined. Transfer mixture to a large bowl.
6. Clean bowl of stand mixer. Using the whisk attachment, beat cream at high speed until stiff peaks form. Fold one-third of whipped cream into peanut butter mixture. Fold in remaining whipped cream.
7. Spread filling onto ganache in crust; refrigerate for 1 hour before serving. Cover and refrigerate for up to 3 days.

1 CUP

BAKED LEMON CURD HAND PIES

Makes 20 hand pies

With prepared lemon curd as a filling, these baked hand pies are a snap to pull together. With their bite-size shape and vanilla-scented glaze, it's hard to resist eating more than one.

All-purpose flour, for dusting
Hand Pie Dough (recipe follows)
1 cup (284 grams) lemon curd
1 large egg (50 grams)
1 tablespoon (15 grams) water
1 cup (120 grams) confectioners' sugar
1 tablespoon (15 grams) whole milk
½ teaspoon (2 grams) vanilla extract

1. Line baking sheets with parchment paper.
2. On a lightly floured surface, roll one portion of Hand Pie Dough into a ⅛-inch-thick circle. Using a 2½-inch round cutter, cut dough, rerolling scraps once. Place 1 inch apart on prepared pans. Top each with 2 teaspoons (6 grams) lemon curd, leaving a ½-inch borderaround edges.
3. On a lightly floured surface, roll remaining Hand Pie Dough into a ⅛-inch-thick circle. Using a 2½-inch round cutter, cut dough, rerolling scraps once.
4. In a small bowl, whisk together egg and 1 tablespoon (15 grams) water; brush onto edges of curd-topped dough circles. Top with remaining dough circles, slightly stretching to cover filling. Press edges of crusts together with a fork to seal. Freeze while oven preheats.
5. Preheat oven to 425°F (220°C).
6. Brush top of dough with egg wash. Using the tip of a paring knife, make a small "X" cut in top of dough.
7. Bake until crust is golden brown, 12 to 14 minutes. Remove from pans, and let cool to room temperature on wire racks.
8. In a small bowl, whisk together confectioners' sugar, milk, and vanilla. Drizzle onto pies. Store in an airtight container for up to 3 days.

Hand Pie Dough

Makes 20 hand pies

2¾ cups (344 grams) all-purpose flour
1 teaspoon (3 grams) kosher salt
1 cup plus 1 tablespoon (241 grams) cold unsalted butter*, cubed
½ cup (120 grams) ice water
2 teaspoons (10 grams) apple cider vinegar

1. In the work bowl of a food processor, pulse flour and salt until combined. Add cold butter, and pulse until mixture is crumbly and butter is pea-size.
2. In a small bowl, combine ½ cup (120 grams) cold water and vinegar. With processor running, add vinegar mixture to flour mixture in a slow, steady stream just until dough comes together. (Mixture will look crumbly, but it should stick together when squeezed between your fingers).
3. Turn out dough, and divide in half. Shape each half into a disk. Wrap in plastic wrap, and refrigerate for 1 hour.

CARAMELIZED ONION AND POTATO GALETTE

Makes 1 (10-inch) galette

This simultaneously rustic and elegant galette is comprised of a buttery herbed crust, creamy garlic cheese, a generous helping of caramelized onions, and thinly sliced potatoes.

---

1 tablespoon (14 grams) unsalted butter
2 cups (240 grams) ¼-inch-sliced sweet onion (about ½ pound)
¾ teaspoon (1.5 grams) kosher salt, divided
⅛ teaspoon granulated sugar
⅛ teaspoon ground black pepper
2 tablespoons (30 grams) dry sherry
12 ounces (340 grams) Yukon gold potatoes (about 3 medium potatoes)
All-purpose flour, for dusting
Thyme Pie Dough (recipe follows)
1 (5.2-ounce) container (150 grams) garlic and herbs spreadable cheese
2 teaspoons (10 grams) canola oil
1 large egg (50 grams), lightly beaten
Garnish: fresh thyme leaves, flaked sea salt

1. In a medium nonstick skillet, melt butter over medium heat. Add onion; cook, stirring occasionally, until softened, 5 to 6 minutes. Add ¼ teaspoon kosher salt, sugar, and pepper; cook, stirring occasionally, until onion is golden brown, 10 to 12 minutes. Add sherry; cook, stirring occasionally, until most of liquid has evaporated. Remove from heat; let cool.
2. Trim ends off potatoes. Slice crosswise ⅛ inch thick. Immediately place in cold water. Let stand for 5 minutes. Drain, pat dry, and place in a medium bowl. Add remaining ½ teaspoon (1.5 grams) kosher salt, and toss until combined.
3. Preheat oven to 425°F (220°C). Line a baking sheet with parchment paper.
4. On a lightly floured surface, roll Thyme Pie Dough into a 14-inch circle. Transfer to prepared pan. (See Note.) Spread cheese in an even layer onto dough, leaving a 1½- to 2-inch border around edges. Sprinkle half of onion (about ¼ cup or 57 grams) onto cheese. Top with potatoes, overlapping and layering as needed. Brush top of potatoes with oil. Fold edges of dough over potatoes. Place remaining onion on top of potatoes. Brush dough with egg.
5. Bake until crust is golden brown, 35 to 45 minutes. Let cool on pan for 10 minutes. Remove from pan, and garnish with thyme and flaked salt, if desired. Serve warm.

Note: *For prettier edges, turn the dough over so the smooth top shows when folding the edges of the dough over the filling.*

THYME PIE DOUGH

Makes 1 (10-inch) crust

½ cup (113 grams) cold unsalted butter, cubed
1½ cups (188 grams) all-purpose flour
1 tablespoon (2 grams) chopped fresh thyme
¾ teaspoon (2.25 grams) kosher salt
⅓ cup (80 grams) ice water

1. Freeze butter for 10 to 15 minutes.
2. In the work bowl of a food processor, pulse flour, thyme, and salt until combined. Add cold butter, and pulse until mixture is crumbly and butter is nickel-size. With processor running, add ⅓ cup (80 grams) ice water in a slow, steady stream just until dough comes together. (Mixture may appear crumbly. It should be moist and hold together when pinched.)
3. Turn out dough, and shape into a disk. Wrap tightly in plastic wrap, and refrigerate for 30 minutes.

APPLE CRUMB PIE

Makes 1 (9-inch) pie

A spice-tinged buttery crumble is not only the crowning glory on top of a towering display of sliced fruit but also doubles as the press-in piecrust.

- 2¼ cups (281 grams) plus ⅓ cup (42 grams) all-purpose flour, divided
- 1¼ cups (250 grams) granulated sugar, divided
- 2½ teaspoons (5 grams) apple pie spice, divided
- 1½ teaspoons (4.5 grams) kosher salt
- ½ cup (113 grams) unsalted butter, melted
- 1 large egg (50 grams), room temperature
- 1 teaspoon (4 grams) vanilla extract
- 7 cups (670 grams) ⅛-inch-sliced Honeycrisp or Pink Lady apples
- 1 tablespoon (15 grams) fresh lemon juice

1. Preheat oven to 350°F (180°C). Spray a 9-inch deep-dish metal pie plate with baking spray with flour.
2. In a large bowl, whisk together 2¼ cups (281 grams) flour, ¾ cup (150 grams) sugar, 1 teaspoon (2 grams) pie spice, and salt. Gradually add melted butter, egg, and vanilla, stirring until just combined and mixture is crumbly. Reserve ¾ cup (165 grams) crumble mixture. Press remaining crumble mixture into bottom and up sides of prepared plate ¼ inch away from top edge. Top with a piece of parchment paper. Add pie weights.
3. Bake until edges are set and center is dry and lightly golden, 6 to 8 minutes. Carefully remove parchment and weights, and bake until surface is dry and set, 3 to 5 minutes more. Let cool on a wire rack for at least 20 minutes. Leave oven on.
4. In another large bowl, stir together apples, lemon juice, remaining ½ cup (100 grams) sugar, remaining ⅓ cup (42 grams) flour, and remaining 1½ teaspoons (3 grams) pie spice. Pile apple mixture into prepared crust. (It will seem like it won't fit in the crust, but use your hands or a spatula to press the apples in to fit.) Top with reserved ¾ cup (165 grams) crumble mixture.
5. Bake until crust is golden brown and apples are tender, about 40 minutes. Let cool completely on a wire rack before serving. Cover and refrigerate for up to 3 days.

BROOKIE PIE

Makes 1 (9-inch) pie

You no longer have to decide between a gloriously soft chocolate chip cookie and a fudgy brownie; this indulgent treat has everything to slake your deepest chocolate craving.

- 6 ounces (170 grams) bittersweet chocolate, chopped
- ½ cup (113 grams) unsalted butter, cubed
- ⅔ cup (147 grams) firmly packed light brown sugar
- ½ cup (100 grams) granulated sugar
- ½ cup (63 grams) all-purpose flour
- 1 tablespoon (5 grams) unsweetened cocoa powder
- 1 teaspoon (3 grams) kosher salt
- ¼ teaspoon instant espresso powder
- 2 large eggs (100 grams), room temperature and lightly beaten
- 1 teaspoon (4 grams) vanilla extract
- Chocolate Chip Cookie Crust (recipe follows)
- Sweetened whipped cream, to serve

1. Preheat oven to 350°F (180°C).
2. In the top of a double boiler, combine chocolate and butter. Cook over simmering water, stirring occasionally, until melted and smooth. Remove from heat, and whisk in sugars until well combined. Let cool slightly, 1 to 2 minutes.
3. In a medium bowl, whisk together flour, cocoa, salt, and espresso powder.
4. Gradually add eggs to chocolate mixture, whisking until combined. Whisk in vanilla. Fold in flour mixture just until combined. Spread batter into Chocolate Chip Cookie Crust.
5. Bake until a wooden pick inserted in center comes out with a few moist crumbs, 55 minutes to 1 hour and 5 minutes. Let cool completely on a wire rack. Serve with whipped cream. Store in an airtight container for up to 3 days.

Chocolate Chip Cookie Crust

Makes 1 (9-inch) crust

- ⅓ cup (73 grams) firmly packed light brown sugar
- ⅓ cup (75 grams) unsalted butter, melted
- 1 large egg (50 grams), room temperature
- 1 teaspoon (4 grams) vanilla extract
- 1¾ cups (219 grams) all-purpose flour
- ½ teaspoon (1.5 grams) kosher salt
- 2 ounces (57 grams) bittersweet chocolate, finely chopped

1. In a large bowl, whisk together brown sugar, melted butter, egg, and vanilla.
2. In a medium bowl, whisk together flour and salt. Gradually add flour mixture to butter mixture, stirring until almost combined. Fold in chocolate until combined and no dry streaks remain.
3. Spray a 9-inch pie plate with baking spray with flour. Press dough into bottom and halfway up sides of prepared plate. Refrigerate until firm, about 30 minutes.

BOUGATSA

Makes 1 (9-inch) pie

This Greek custard pie is a crisp, creamy treat found at nearly every corner bakery and café in Greece. Made with flaky layers of phyllo surrounding a velvety vanilla and cinnamon custard, this classic breakfast treat is dusted with confectioners' sugar for a touch of sweet spice and contrast to the gorgeously golden phyllo below.

¾ cup (150 grams) granulated sugar, divided
4 large eggs (200 grams), room temperature
6 tablespoons (48 grams) cornstarch
1½ teaspoons (4.5 grams) kosher salt
3 cups (720 grams) whole milk, room temperature
2 teaspoons (8 grams) vanilla extract
1½ teaspoons (3 grams) ground cinnamon
12 to 15 sheets (150 to 188 grams) frozen phyllo pastry, thawed according to package directions
½ cup (113 grams) unsalted butter, melted
Garnish: confectioners' sugar, ground cinnamon

1. In a medium bowl, whisk together ½ cup (100 grams) granulated sugar, eggs, cornstarch, and salt.
2. In a small saucepan, whisk together milk and remaining ¼ cup (50 grams) granulated sugar. Heat over medium-high heat, stirring frequently, until steaming, 4 to 5 minutes. (Do not boil.) Slowly add half of hot milk mixture to egg mixture, whisking constantly. Add egg mixture to remaining hot milk mixture in pan; whisk in vanilla and cinnamon. Bring to a boil, whisking constantly; cook, whisking constantly; for 2 minutes. Remove from heat, and strain through a fine-mesh sieve, discarding any solids.
3. Preheat oven to 375°F (190°C). Line a 9-inch square baking pan with parchment paper, letting excess extend over sides of pan.
4. Lay 1 sheet of phyllo in prepared pan so it covers bottom of pan and hangs over one edge of pan; brush with melted butter. Place another sheet of phyllo directly on top. Repeat procedure with 2 more sheets of phyllo but hanging over edge of opposite side of pan. Repeat procedure for final two sides of pan for a total of 8 sheets stacked, 2 sheets per side. Pour custard into phyllo; fold excess phyllo over to envelop custard. Brush top with melted butter. Scrunch and crinkle remaining sheets of phyllo to create folds and waves, and place on top of pie, covering entire surface. (Rip or tear sheets as needed.) Drizzle remaining melted butter on top of pie.
5. Bake until phyllo is golden brown, 25 to 30 minutes. Let cool in pan for at least 15 minutes. Using excess parchment as handles, remove from pan. Just before serving, garnish with confectioners' sugar and cinnamon, if desired. Best served warm.

SWEET POTATO TART

Makes 1 (9½-inch) tart

A twist on the classic sweet potato pie, our tart has a gingery cookie crust topped with spiced sweet potato filling and dolloped with a billowy marshmallow meringue.

1⅓ cups (202 grams) firmly packed finely crushed Biscoff Cookies (about 26 cookies)
¼ cup (57 grams) unsalted butter, melted
1¼ teaspoons (2.5 grams) ground cinnamon, divided
½ teaspoon kosher salt, divided
5 ounces (142 grams) cream cheese, room temperature
1¼ cups (295 grams) mashed cooked peeled sweet potato
½ cup (110 grams) firmly packed light brown sugar
2 teaspoons (6 grams) all-purpose flour
¾ teaspoon (4.5 grams) vanilla bean paste
½ teaspoon (1 gram) ground ginger
⅛ teaspoon ground cloves
2 large eggs (100 grams), room temperature
Vanilla Bean Meringue (recipe follows)

1. Preheat oven to 350°F (180°C). Spray a 9½-inch round fluted removable-bottom tart pan with baking spray with flour.
2. In a large bowl, stir together crushed cookies, melted butter, ½ teaspoon (1 gram) cinnamon, and ¼ teaspoon salt until well combined; using the bottom of a measuring cup, press crumb mixture into bottom and up sides of prepared pan.
3. Bake until set and fragrant, 8 to 10 minutes. Let cool completely on a wire rack. Reduce oven temperature to 325°F (170°C).
4. In the bowl of a stand mixer fitted with the paddle attachment, beat cream cheese at medium speed until smooth and creamy, about 2 minutes, stopping to scrape sides of bowl. Add sweet potato, brown sugar, flour, vanilla bean paste, ginger, cloves, remaining ¾ teaspoon (1.5 grams) cinnamon, and remaining ¼ teaspoon salt; beat until well combined, about 2 minutes, stopping to scrape paddle and bottom and sides of bowl. Add eggs, one at a time, beating until well combined after each addition and stopping to scrape sides of bowl. (Mixture will be on the thicker side.) Spread filling into prepared crust.
5. Bake until top of filling is set and an instant-read thermometer inserted in center registers 155°F (68°C), 22 to 28 minutes. Let cool completely in pan on a wire rack.
6. Carefully remove tart from pan; transfer to a serving plate. Spoon and spread Vanilla Bean Meringue onto tart as desired. Using a handheld kitchen torch, carefully brown meringue as desired. Serve immediately. Cover and refrigerate for up to 2 days.

Vanilla Bean Meringue

Makes about 5 cups

1¼ cups (250 grams) granulated sugar
6 large egg whites (180 grams), room temperature
¼ teaspoon (1 gram) cream of tartar
¼ teaspoon kosher salt
2 teaspoons (12 grams) vanilla bean paste

1. In the heatproof bowl of a stand mixer, whisk together sugar, egg whites, cream of tartar, and salt. Place over a saucepan of simmering water, and cook, stirring frequently, until an instant-read thermometer registers 160°F (71°C), 15 to 20 minutes.
2. Return bowl to stand mixer. Using the whisk attachment, beat sugar mixture at medium-high speed until bowl is room temperature and meringue forms glossy, stiff peaks, about 10 minutes. Beat in vanilla paste. Use immediately.

BALANCE

CREAMY SPINACH GALETTE

Makes 1 (10-inch) galette

Fresh spinach, bold garlic, and a richly seasoned crust create a winning combination in this brunch-worthy galette.

---

2 tablespoons (28 grams) unsalted butter
3 cloves garlic (9 grams), minced
4 cups (135 grams) roughly chopped fresh baby spinach
½ cup (120 grams) heavy whipping cream
2 tablespoons (16 grams) all-purpose flour, plus more for dusting
1 teaspoon (3 grams) kosher salt
Cheesy Crust (recipe follows)
1 large egg (50 grams), lightly beaten
Garnish: crushed red pepper

1. Preheat oven to 400°F (200°C). Line a large rimmed baking sheet with parchment paper.
2. In a large skillet, melt butter over medium heat. Add garlic; cook until fragrant, about 30 seconds. Add spinach in batches, stirring frequently, until slightly wilted, about 2 minutes. Stir in cream, flour, and salt; cook until slightly thickened, about 2 minutes. Remove from heat; let cool.
3. On a lightly floured surface, roll Cheesy Piecrust into a 12-inch circle, about ¼ inch thick. Transfer to prepared pan. Using a fork, prick dough all over in ½-inch intervals. Spread cooled spinach mixture into an eve layer on dough, leaving a 1-inch border around edges. Fold edges over spinach mixture in 2-inch sections, overlapping and pinching to seal gaps. Brush egg onto crust.
4. Bake until top of filling looks dry and edges of crust are lightly browned, 12 to 15 minutes. Rotate pan, and reduce oven temperature to 350°F (180°C). Bake until crust is golden brown, 5 to 8 minutes more. Let cool on pan for 10 minutes. Garnish with red pepper, if desired. Serve warm.

Cheesy Crust

Makes 1 (10-inch) crust

1½ cups (188 grams) all-purpose flour, plus more for dusting
½ teaspoon (1.5 grams) kosher salt
¼ teaspoon dry mustard
⅛ teaspoon smoked paprika
⅛ teaspoon ground black pepper
½ cup (113 grams) cold unsalted butter, cubed
½ cup (57 grams) shredded Gouda cheese
½ cup (57 grams) shredded extra-sharp white Cheddar cheese
¼ cup (60 grams) ice water

1. In the work bowl of a food processor, pulse together flour, salt, dry mustard, paprika, and pepper. Add cold butter and cheeses; pulse until mixture is crumbly. With processor running, add ¼ cup (60 grams) ice water, 1 tablespoon (15 grams) at a time, just until dough comes together.
2. Turn out dough onto a heavily floured surface, and shape into a disk. Wrap in plastic wrap, and refrigerate for 45 minutes.

COOKIES AND BARS

Whether you're craving a rich, gooey brownie, a fruit-filled cookie, or something in between, these easy recipes deliver every time

CHOCOLATE-ALMOND BISCOTTI

Makes about 20 biscotti

These oil-based biscotti are based on a southern Italian family recipe. Using oil rather than butter creates a more tender crumb, even with the two bakes. Drizzle with or dip the cookies into melted chocolate and sprinkle with chopped almonds for a final flourish.

¾ cup (150 grams) granulated sugar
2 large eggs (100 grams), room temperature
⅓ cup (75 grams) neutral oil
¾ teaspoon (3 grams) almond extract
¼ teaspoon (1 gram) vanilla extract
2 cups (250 grams) all-purpose flour
2 teaspoons (10 grams) baking powder
1 teaspoon (3 grams) kosher salt
¾ cup (110 grams) almonds, roughly chopped
4 ounces (113 grams) semisweet chocolate, chopped
Garnish: finely chopped almonds

1. Preheat oven to 350°F (180°C). Line a baking sheet with parchment paper.
2. In a large bowl, whisk together sugar and eggs until thick and combined. Slowly add oil, whisking until combined; whisk in extracts.
3. In a medium bowl, whisk together flour, baking powder, and salt. Add flour mixture to sugar mixture, folding until almost combined. Add roughly chopped almonds, and fold until combined and no dry streaks remain. Spoon dough onto prepared pan, and shape into a 9x3-inch loaf (about ¾ inch thick).
4. Bake until firm and edges are lightly golden, about 35 minutes. Let cool on pan enough to handle, about 20 minutes. Leave oven on.
5. Transfer loaf to a cutting board. Line baking sheet with a new sheet of parchment. Using a sharp serrated knife, carefully slice loaf into ¾-inch-thick slices. Place, cut side down, on prepared pan.
6. Bake until dry and edges are golden, 15 to 20 minutes, turning biscotti halfway through baking. Let cool completely on pan.
7. In a tall microwave-safe bowl or liquid-measuring cup, heat chocolate on high in 30-second intervals, stirring between each, until almost completely melted. Stir until melted and smooth. Dip ends of cooled biscotti into melted chocolate, and place on parchment paper. Garnish with finely chopped almonds, if desired. (Alternatively, transfer melted chocolate to a pastry bag, and cut a ⅛-inch opening in tip; drizzle chocolate onto biscotti as desired.) Let stand until chocolate is set. Store in an airtight container for up to 1 week.

pro tip

For the softer, once-baked unscotti, prepare the loaf as directed through baking in step 4. Let cool completely on the pan, and transfer to a cutting board. Slice into ¾-inch-thick cookies. Store in an airtight container for up to 1 week.

STRAWBERRY PRETZEL THUMBPRINT COOKIES

Makes 20 cookies

There's something almost nostalgic about the combination of crunchy pretzels, jammy strawberries, and tangy cream cheese. It'll be nearly impossible to eat just one of these chewy-creamy-crispy cookies.

¾ cup (170 grams) unsalted butter, softened
½ cup (100 grams) granulated sugar
1 large egg (50 grams), room temperature
2 teaspoons (8 grams) vanilla extract
2 cups (250 grams) all-purpose flour
¾ teaspoon (2.25 grams) kosher salt
4 cups (128 grams) lightly crushed pretzels
⅔ cup (180 grams) Quick Strawberry Jam (recipe follows)
Cream Cheese Glaze (recipe follows)

1. Preheat oven to 350°F (180°C). Line baking sheets with parchment paper.
2. In the bowl of a stand mixer fitted with the paddle attachment, beat butter and sugar at medium speed until pale and creamy, 3 to 4 minutes, stopping to scrape sides of bowl. Add egg and vanilla, beating until combined.
3. In a small bowl, whisk together flour and salt. With mixer on low speed, gradually add flour mixture to butter mixture, beating until just combined and stopping to scrape sides of bowl.
4. In a shallow bowl, place pretzels.
5. Using a 1½-tablespoon spring-loaded scoop, scoop dough, and roll into balls. Roll in pretzels, slightly pressing with your hands as needed to make sure pretzels adhere. Place at least 1½ inches apart on prepared pans. Using your thumb, gently make an indentation in center of each ball. Refrigerate until firm, at least 15 minutes.
6. Bake until set and edges are lightly browned, 10 to 12 minutes. Immediately press down centers. Let cool on pans for 10 minutes. Remove from pans, and let cool completely on a wire rack.
7. Spoon 1½ teaspoons (9 grams) Quick Strawberry Jam into center of each cooled cookie. Drizzle Cream Cheese Glaze onto cookies. Refrigerate in an airtight container for up to 3 days.

QUICK STRAWBERRY JAM

Makes about 1½ cups

1 pound (454 grams) fresh strawberries, hulled and chopped
2¼ cups (250 grams) granulated sugar
2 tablespoons (30 grams) fresh lemon juice

1. In a small saucepan, bring all ingredients to a boil over medium-high heat, stirring occasionally. Reduce heat to low; cook, stirring frequently, until mixture is thick, 25 to 30 minutes. Transfer to a shallow dish, and let cool completely. Refrigerate in an airtight container for up to 3 weeks.

CREAM CHEESE GLAZE

Makes about ¾ cup

4 ounces (113 grams) cream cheese, softened
¼ cup (30 grams) confectioners' sugar
2 tablespoons (30 grams) whole milk

1. In a small bowl, whisk together all ingredients until smooth.

CONFETTI BARS

Makes 24 bars

I never need a reason to bake with sprinkles, and where there are sprinkles, there is a celebration! Whether it's a birthday, graduation, anniversary, or a Wednesday, these fun bars will always put a smile on your face.

- 1 cup (227 grams) unsalted butter, softened
- 1 cup (225 grams) cream cheese, softened
- 1½ cups (300 grams) granulated sugar
- 1 large egg (50 grams), room temperature
- 2 teaspoons (8 grams) vanilla extract
- ½ teaspoon (2 grams) almond extract
- 2½ cups (313 grams) all-purpose flour
- ½ teaspoon (2.5 grams) baking powder
- ½ teaspoon (1.5 grams) kosher salt
- 1 cup (183 grams) rainbow sprinkles
- Confectioners' sugar, for dusting

1. Preheat oven to 350°F (180°C). Line a 13x9-inch baking pan with parchment paper, letting excess extend over sides of pan. Lightly spray paper with cooking spray.
2. In the bowl of a stand mixer fitted with the paddle attachment, beat butter, cream cheese, and granulated sugar at medium speed until creamy, 2 to 3 minutes, stopping to scrape paddle and bottom and sides of bowl. Add egg and extracts, beating until combined.
3. In a medium bowl, whisk together flour, baking powder, and salt. Add flour mixture to butter mixture, beating on low speed until combined. (Dough will be thick.) Stir in sprinkles. Spread dough into prepared pan using a metal spatula.
4. Bake until center is set, 20 to 30 minutes. Let cool in pan for 15 minutes. Using excess parchment as handles, remove from pan, and let cool completely on a wire rack.
5. Cut into bars; dust with confectioners' sugar just before serving. Store in an airtight container for up to 3 days.

pro tip

Stirring in the sprinkles ensures they don't break into pieces.

BLACK-AND-WHITE COOKIES

Makes about 12 cookies

Also called half-moon cookies, these cakey treats have a bright, tender base thanks to sour cream and lemon zest. A subtle vanilla glaze goes toe-to-toe with a rich ganache, melding two delicious icings to create one stunning whole.

½ cup (113 grams) unsalted butter, room temperature
¾ cup (150 grams) granulated sugar
2 large eggs (100 grams), room temperature
2 cups (250 grams) all-purpose flour
1 teaspoon (5 grams) baking powder
¾ teaspoon (2.25 grams) kosher salt
¼ cup (60 grams) sour cream, room temperature
¼ cup (60 grams) whole milk, room temperature
2 teaspoons (8 grams) vanilla extract
1 teaspoon (3 grams) tightly packed lemon zest
Vanilla Glaze (recipe follows)
Chocolate Ganache (recipe follows)

1. Preheat oven to 375°F (190°C). Line 2 rimmed baking pans with parchment paper.
2. In the bowl of a stand mixer fitted with the paddle attachment, beat butter and sugar at medium speed until light and fluffy, 3 to 4 minutes, stopping to scrape sides of bowl. Add eggs, one at a time, beating well after each addition and stopping to scrape sides of bowl.
3. In a medium bowl, whisk together flour, baking powder, and salt. In another medium bowl, whisk together sour cream, milk, vanilla, and lemon zest. With mixer on low speed, gradually add flour mixture to butter mixture alternately with sour cream mixture, beginning and ending with flour mixture, beating just until combined after each addition.
4. Using a ¼-cup spring-loaded scoop, scoop batter, and place 2 inches apart on prepared pans. Lightly bang pans on a kitchen towel-lined counter to help batter spread.
5. Bake until edges are lightly browned, about 12 minutes, rotating pans halfway through baking. (See Notes.) (Be careful not to overbake or cookies will dry out.) Let cool on pans for 15 minutes. Remove from pans, and let cool completely on wire racks.
6. Spoon Vanilla Glaze into a squeeze bottle. (See Notes.)
7. Place cooled cookies flat side up. Pipe a line of Vanilla Glaze down center and around edge of half of each cookie, creating a semicircle. Fill in center with glaze, and smooth with an offset spatula. Let stand until dry, about 15 minutes.
8. Carefully pour Chocolate Ganache into a squeeze bottle. Pipe and fill in on opposite side of each cookie with ganache, smoothing with an offset spatula. Let dry completely, about 30 minutes.

Notes: *A large round cutter can be used when rotating pans halfway through baking to form the cookies into a more circular shape, if desired. Place cutter around 1 batter round; gently move cutter in a circular motion while making contact with edges of batter until desired shape is reached. Repeat as needed.*

If you do not have squeeze bottles, spoon Vanilla Glaze and Chocolate Ganache into separate pastry bags fitted with a ⅛-inch round piping tip.

Vanilla Glaze

Makes about ½ cup

1 cup (120 grams) confectioners' sugar
1 tablespoon (21 grams) light corn syrup
¼ teaspoon (1 gram) vanilla extract
2 to 4 tablespoons (30 to 60 grams) cold heavy whipping cream

1. In medium bowl, stir together confectioners' sugar, corn syrup, and vanilla. Gradually stir in cold cream until mixture is smooth and thick and falls off a spatula in sections of thick ribbon. Use immediately.

Chocolate Ganache

Makes about ¾ cup

5 ounces (142 grams) bittersweet chocolate, chopped
¼ cup (57 grams) unsalted butter

1. In the top of a double boiler, combine chocolate and butter. Cook over simmering water, stirring occasionally, until melted and smooth.

CHEWY CHOCOLATE CHIP COOKIES

Makes about 36 cookies

This chocolate-laden creation stays moist and flexible for days after baking—perfect for folks who want no resistance when sinking their teeth into a cookie.

- ¾ cup (170 grams) European-style unsalted butter, melted
- 1 cup (220 grams) firmly packed light brown sugar
- ⅔ cup (133 grams) granulated sugar
- 1 large egg (50 grams)
- 1 large egg yolk (19 grams)
- 1 tablespoon (18 grams) vanilla bean paste
- 2 cups (250 grams) all-purpose flour
- ⅓ cup (42 grams) bread flour
- 2 teaspoons (6 grams) cornstarch
- ¾ teaspoon (3.75 grams) baking soda
- ¾ teaspoon (2.25 grams) kosher salt
- 1½ cups (255 grams) semisweet chocolate chips

Garnish: flaked salt

1. Preheat oven to 350°F (180°C). Line rimmed baking sheets with parchment paper.

2. In the bowl of a stand mixer fitted with the paddle attachment, beat melted butter and sugars at medium speed until fluffy, 3 to 4 minutes, stopping to scrape sides of bowl. Reduce mixer speed to medium-low. Add egg and egg yolk, one at a time, beating well after each addition. Beat in vanilla bean paste.

3. In a medium bowl, whisk together flours, cornstarch, baking soda, and kosher salt. With mixer on low speed, gradually add flour mixture to butter mixture, beating just until combined. (Do not overmix.) Gently stir in chocolate.

4. Using a 1-tablespoon spring-loaded scoop, scoop two-thirds of dough, and drop dough 2 inches apart onto prepared pans. Using a 1½-teaspoon spring-loaded scoop, scoop dough, and place on top of each larger piece of dough. Lightly press dough pieces together.

5. Bake, one pan at a time, until edges are lightly browned and tops still look a little gooey, 9 to 10 minutes, rotating pans halfway through baking. Let cool on pans for 5 minutes. Garnish with flaked salt, if desired.

6. Remove from pans, and let cool completely on wire racks. Store in an airtight container for up to 3 days.

WHITE CHOCOLATE-FRUITY CEREAL COOKIES

Makes about 32 cookies

These whimsically bright and fruity cookies are the ultimate combination of tender, chewy cookie dough, multicolored fruity cereal, sweet white chocolate chunks, and a touch of cardamom to add a zesty, almost citrusy kick. The best accompaniment to this cookie? A cool glass of milk, of course!

½ cup (113 grams) unsalted butter, softened
½ cup (100 grams) granulated sugar
½ cup (110 grams) firmly packed dark brown sugar
2 large eggs (100 grams)
1 tablespoon (13 grams) vanilla extract
2¼ cups (281 grams) all-purpose flour
1¾ teaspoons (6 grams) baking powder
1½ teaspoons (4.5 grams) kosher salt
½ teaspoon (1 gram) ground cardamom
¼ teaspoon (1.25 grams) baking soda
2 cups (340 grams) chopped white chocolate
1 cup (50 grams) finely crushed sweetened O-shaped fruit-flavored cereal
1 cup (38 grams) roughly crushed sweetened O-shaped fruit-flavored cereal

1. Preheat oven to 350°F (180°C). Line 2 rimmed baking sheets with parchment paper.
2. In the bowl of a stand mixer fitted with the paddle attachment, beat butter and sugars at medium speed until fluffy, 3 to 4 minutes, stopping to scrape sides of bowl. Add eggs, one at a time, beating until combined after each addition. Beat in vanilla.
3. In a medium bowl, whisk together flour, baking powder, salt, cardamom, and baking soda. With mixer on low speed, gradually add flour mixture to butter mixture, beating until combined. Add white chocolate and finely crushed cereal, and beat until combined.
4. In a small shallow bowl, place roughly crushed cereal.
5. Using a 2-tablespoon spring-loaded scoop, scoop dough (about 53 grams each), and roll into balls; roll in cereal. Place about 1½ inches apart on prepared pans.
6. Bake until slightly domed and thick and edges are golden brown, 10 to 11 minutes. Let cool on pans for 5 minutes. Remove from pans, and let cool completely on a wire rack. Store in an airtight container for up to 5 days.

GRAPE JELLY-STUFFED PEANUT BUTTER COOKIES

Makes about 15 cookies

Chewy honey- and brown sugar-sweetened peanut butter cookie dough is filled with tangy grape jelly, sprinkled with turbinado sugar and baked to golden perfection. Complete with a sugary crunch, nutty peanut flavor, and a jammy center, these cookies are a PB&J lover's dream.

- ½ cup (113 grams) unsalted butter, softened
- 1 cup (220 grams) firmly packed light brown sugar
- 1 large egg (50 grams), room temperature
- 2 large egg yolks (37 grams), room temperature
- ¾ cup (192 grams) creamy peanut butter
- 1 tablespoon (21 grams) honey
- 1 teaspoon (4 grams) vanilla extract
- 2¼ cups (281 grams) all-purpose flour
- 1 teaspoon (5 grams) baking powder
- ¼ teaspoon (1.25 grams) baking soda
- ¾ cup (240 grams) grape jelly
- ½ cup (100 grams) turbinado sugar

1. In the bowl of a stand mixer fitted with the paddle attachment, beat butter and brown sugar at medium speed until fluffy, 3 to 4 minutes, stopping to scrape sides of bowl. Add egg and egg yolks, beating until well combined. Beat in peanut butter, honey, and vanilla.
2. In a large bowl, whisk together flour, baking powder, and baking soda. With mixer on low speed, gradually add flour mixture to butter mixture, beating just until combined. Cover and refrigerate for 1 hour.
3. Preheat oven to 325°F (170°C). Line baking sheets with parchment paper.
4. Using a 1½-tablespoon spring-loaded scoop, scoop dough (about 30 grams each), roll into balls, and flatten into 2½-inch disks.
5. Spoon 2 teaspoons (14 grams) jelly in center of 1 dough disk, and cover with a second disk. Crimp edges to seal, and gently shape edges to be smooth and rounded. (See Note.) Place completed dough disk about 2½ inches apart on prepared pan.
6. Repeat with remaining jelly and remaining dough disks. Sprinkle all dough disks with turbinado sugar, lightly pressing into tops.
7. Bake until bottoms are golden brown and tops look dry, 10 to 14 minutes, rotating pans halfway through baking. Let cool completely on pans on wire racks. Store in an airtight container for up to 3 days.

Note: *Work one at a time so the jelly doesn't slide when you aren't looking. Place the jelly-sandwiched disks in your hand to crimp and use your palm to cup the sides and shape them so they're smooth and rounded to minimize cracking.*

APPLE-STREUSEL COOKIES

Makes 24 cookies

If apple crisp became a cookie, this would be it. Each cookie is loaded with fresh fruit and a blend of warm spices, but it's the streusel and glaze that evoke all the best fall feelings.

½ cup (113 grams) unsalted butter, softened
1 cup (200 grams) granulated sugar
½ cup (110 grams) firmly packed light brown sugar
2 large eggs (100 grams), room temperature
1½ teaspoons (6 grams) vanilla extract
3 cups (375 grams) all-purpose flour
1 teaspoon (5 grams) baking soda
1 teaspoon (3 grams) kosher salt
½ teaspoon (1 gram) ground cinnamon
¼ teaspoon ground nutmeg
¼ teaspoon ground allspice
1¼ cups (140 grams) ¼-inch-diced Pink Lady apples
Oat Streusel (recipe follows)
Spiced Glaze (recipe follows)

1. Preheat oven to 375°F (190°C). Line baking sheets with parchment paper.
2. In the bowl of a stand mixer fitted with the paddle attachment, beat butter and sugars at medium speed until fluffy, 3 to 4 minutes, stopping to scrape sides of bowl. Add eggs, one at a time, beating well after each addition. Beat in vanilla.
3. In a medium bowl, whisk together flour, baking soda, salt, cinnamon, nutmeg, and allspice. With mixer on low speed, gradually add flour mixture to butter mixture, beating until just a few streaks of flour remain. Add apples, and beat just until combined. Using a 2-tablespoon spring-loaded scoop, scoop dough (about 36 grams each), and place 2 inches apart on prepared pans.
4. Bake, one pan at a time, until dough begins to soften, about 4 minutes. Sprinkle 2 teaspoons (about 7 grams) Oat Streusel on each parbaked cookie, and gently press into top. Bake until streusel and edges of cookies are lightly browned, 6 to 8 minutes more. Let cool completely on pans on wire racks. Drizzle Spiced Glaze onto cooled cookies. Store in an airtight container for up to 3 days.

Oat Streusel

Makes about 1 cup

½ cup (40 grams) old-fashioned oats
¼ cup (31 grams) all-purpose flour
3 tablespoons (42 grams) firmly packed light brown sugar
¼ teaspoon kosher salt
¼ teaspoon ground cinnamon
⅛ teaspoon ground nutmeg
⅛ teaspoon ground allspice
2 tablespoons (28 grams) cold unsalted butter, cubed

1. In a medium bowl, whisk together oats, flour, brown sugar, salt, cinnamon, nutmeg, and allspice. Using a pastry blender or 2 forks, cut in cold butter until butter is pea-size. Pinch and rub pieces of butter into dry ingredients with fingertips until mixture comes together. Freeze for 10 minutes before using.

Spiced Glaze

Makes about ⅓ cup

1 cup (120 grams) confectioners' sugar
2 tablespoons (30 grams) whole milk
¼ teaspoon ground cinnamon

1. In a small bowl, whisk together all ingredients until smooth. Use immediately.

SNICKERDOODLES

Makes 38 cookies

If you've been searching for the ultimate snickerdoodle, you found it. An enduring classic, this cookie is the pinnacle of chewy, tangy, and richly spiced magic.

- 1 cup (227 grams) unsalted butter, softened
- 1¾ cups (350 grams) granulated sugar, divided
- ½ cup (110 grams) firmly packed light brown sugar
- 2 large eggs (100 grams), room temperature
- 1½ teaspoons (6 grams) vanilla extract
- 2¾ cups (344 grams) all-purpose flour
- 1½ teaspoons (4.5 grams) cream of tartar
- 1 teaspoon (5 grams) baking soda
- 1 teaspoon (3 grams) kosher salt
- 2½ teaspoons (5 grams) ground cinnamon

1. Preheat oven to 400°F (200°C). Line baking sheets with parchment paper.

2. In the bowl of a stand mixer fitted with the paddle attachment, beat butter, 1¼ cups (250 grams) granulated sugar, and brown sugar at medium speed until fluffy, 3 to 4 minutes, stopping to scrape sides of bowl. Add eggs, one at a time, beating well after each addition. Beat in vanilla.

3. In a medium bowl, whisk together flour, cream of tartar, baking soda, and salt. With mixer on low speed, gradually add flour mixture to butter mixture, beating just until combined.

4. In another medium bowl, stir together cinnamon and remaining ½ cup (100 grams) granulated sugar.

5. Using a 1½-tablespoon spring-loaded scoop, scoop dough (28 to 30 grams each), and roll into smooth 1½-inch balls. Toss in cinnamon sugar until well coated. Place 2 inches apart on prepared pans.

6. Bake, one pan at a time, until edges are lightly browned but centers still look a little gooey, 8 to 10 minutes. Let cool on pan for 5 minutes. Remove from pans, and let cool completely on wire racks. Store in an airtight container for up to 3 days.

SOFT AMARETTI COOKIES

Makes about 28 cookies

Derived from the Italian word for "bitter" (amaro)*, almond-rich amaretti cookies originated in Italy in the Middle Ages. Though they can often be crunchy like biscotti, these crinkly cookies promise a soft, chewy crumb and unparalleled sweet almond flavor.*

---

10 ounces (284 grams) blanched almonds (about 1¾ cups), lightly toasted (see Notes)
1¼ cups (250 grams) granulated sugar, divided
¾ cup (90 grams) confectioners' sugar, divided
¾ teaspoon (2.25 grams) kosher salt
2 large egg whites (60 grams), room temperature
¾ teaspoon (3 grams) almond extract
¾ teaspoon (3 grams) vanilla extract

1. Preheat oven to 300°F (150°C). Line 2 baking sheets with parchment paper.
2. In the work bowl of a food processor, pulse almonds and ¾ cup (150 grams) granulated sugar until almonds are finely ground, stopping to scrape sides of bowl. Add ¼ cup (30 grams) confectioners' sugar and salt; pulse until combined. Add egg whites, one at a time, pulsing until combined after each addition. Add extracts; pulse just until a dough forms.
3. In a small wide bowl, place remaining ½ cup (100 grams) granulated sugar. In another small wide bowl, place remaining ½ cup (60 grams) confectioners' sugar.
4. Scoop dough by tablespoonfuls (about 18 grams each), and roll into balls. Roll dough balls in granulated sugar; roll in confectioners' sugar. Place 1 to 1½ inches apart on prepared pans.
5. Bake, one pan at a time, until tops are cracked, bottoms are golden, and edges are set but still give slightly when pressed, 20 to 24 minutes, rotating pan halfway through baking. Let cool on pan for 5 minutes. Remove from pan, and let cool completely on wire racks. Store in an airtight container for up to 3 days.

Notes: *If you can't find blanched almonds, you can always blanch your own. In a large heatproof bowl, cover desired amount of almonds with boiling water. Let stand for 1 minute; thoroughly drain in a fine-mesh sieve, and run under cold water. Pinch, peel off, and discard almond skins. Pat blanched almonds completely dry before prepping as directed.*

To toast, bake blanched almonds at 350°F (180°C) until lightly browned, 4 to 7 minutes, stirring occasionally.

SAGE, ASIAGO, AND PECAN SHORTBREAD COINS

Makes 24 cookies

This cheesy, herbaceous take on classic shortbread will be the MVP of your next charcuterie board. Asiago cheese imparts a salty zing that's complemented by the woody notes of sage, resulting in a savory snack reminiscent of the flavors of the Mediterranean.

½ cup (113 grams) unsalted butter, softened
1 cup (99 grams) packed finely shredded Asiago cheese
2 tablespoons (14 grams) finely chopped pecans
1 teaspoon minced fresh sage
½ teaspoon (1.5 grams) kosher salt
½ teaspoon (1 gram) ground black pepper
1¼ cups (156 grams) all-purpose flour
1 large egg white (30 grams), beaten
Pecan halves and fresh sage leaves (optional)

1. In the bowl of a stand mixer fitted with the paddle attachment, beat butter at medium speed until creamy, about 1 minute. Add Asiago, chopped pecans, minced sage, salt, and pepper, beating until combined. With mixer on low speed, gradually add flour, beating until large clumps form, 2 to 3 minutes.

2. Turn out dough onto a work surface, and gently knead until no longer crumbly. Shape into a 9½-inch-long log. Wrap in plastic wrap, and freeze until firm, about 1 hour.

3. Preheat oven to 350°F (180°C). Line a baking sheet with parchment paper.

4. Using a serrated knife, cut log into 24 (⅜-inch-thick) slices. Place about 1 inch apart on prepared pan. Brush with egg white. Top with pecan halves and sage leaves, if desired.

5. Bake until lightly browned on the bottom, 18 to 20 minutes. Let cool completely on pan on a wire rack. Store in an airtight container for up to 2 weeks.

LEMON CRUMB BARS

Makes 16 bars

A simple stir-together filling is layered between a spiced-infused crust and crumb topping, which complements the tangy fruit flavor.

- ½ cup (113 grams) unsalted butter, softened
- ¾ cup (165 grams) firmly packed light brown sugar
- 1¼ cups (156 grams) all-purpose flour
- ¾ cup (78 grams) quick-cooking oats
- 1 tablespoon (9 grams) plus 1 teaspoon (3 grams) tightly packed lemon zest, divided
- ¾ teaspoon (1.5 grams) kosher salt, divided
- ½ teaspoon (2.5 grams) baking powder
- ½ teaspoon (1 gram) ground cardamom
- 1 (14-ounce) can (396 grams) sweetened condensed milk
- ⅔ cup (160 grams) fresh lemon juice
- 3 large egg yolks (56 grams)

1. Preheat oven to 350°F (180°C). Spray an 8-inch square baking pan with baking spray with flour. Line pan with parchment paper, letting excess extend over sides of pan.

2. In the bowl of a stand mixer fitted with the paddle attachment, beat butter and brown sugar at medium speed until fluffy, 3 to 4 minutes, stopping to scrape sides of bowl.

3. In a medium bowl, whisk together flour, oats, 1 teaspoon (3 grams) lemon zest, ½ teaspoon (1.5 grams) salt, baking powder, and cardamom. With mixer on low speed, gradually add flour mixture to butter mixture, beating until combined. (Mixture will be crumbly.) Firmly press two-thirds of mixture (about 2 packed cups or 350 grams) into bottom of prepared pan. Cover and refrigerate remaining mixture until ready to use.

4. Bake until slightly puffed and edges are dry, about 15 minutes. Let cool in pan on a wire rack for 15 minutes. Leave oven on.

5. In a large bowl, whisk together condensed milk, lemon juice, egg yolks, remaining 1 tablespoon (9 grams) lemon zest, and remaining ¼ teaspoon salt. Spread filling onto prepared crust. Sprinkle with reserved crumble mixture.

6. Bake until center is just set and crumble is lightly browned, about 40 minutes, rotating pan halfway through baking. Let cool completely in pan on a wire rack. Using excess parchment as handles, remove from pan, and cut into bars. Refrigerate in an airtight container for up to 3 days.

TRIPLE-CITRUS SHEET PAN SHORTBREAD

Makes 18 to 20 cookies

Somewhere between a cookie and a bar, sheet pan shortbread is a total game changer. For this triple-citrus take, grapefruit, orange, and lime zests are incorporated into the buttery, rich shortbread and the glaze for a light and lovely pop of flavor. It'll be impossible to resist slicing into and snacking on this sweet and simple treat throughout the day.

1½ cups (340 grams) unsalted butter, softened
1 cup (200 grams) granulated sugar
2 teaspoons (6 grams) tightly packed grapefruit zest
2 teaspoons (6 grams) tightly packed lime zest
2 teaspoons (6 grams) tightly packed orange zest
4 cups (500 grams) all-purpose flour
¼ cup (32 grams) cornstarch
¾ teaspoon (1.5 grams) kosher salt, divided
2 cups (240 grams) confectioners' sugar, sifted
2 tablespoons (28 grams) unsalted butter, melted
1 tablespoon (15 grams) fresh grapefruit juice
1 tablespoon (15 grams) fresh lime juice
1 tablespoon (15 grams) fresh orange juice
Garnish: grapefruit zest, lime zest, orange zest

1. Preheat oven to 325°F (170°C). Spray an 18x13-inch rimmed baking sheet with baking spray with flour. Line pan with parchment paper, letting excess extend over sides of pan.

2. In the bowl of a stand mixer fitted with the paddle attachment, beat softened butter, granulated sugar, grapefruit zest, lime zest, and orange zest at medium speed until creamy, 3 to 4 minutes, stopping to scrape sides of bowl.

3. In a medium bowl, whisk together flour, cornstarch, and ½ teaspoon (1.5 grams) salt. With mixer on low speed, gradually add flour mixture to butter mixture, beating until dough comes together. Dollop dough onto prepared pan. Press dough evenly into pan. (If dough gets too warm and sticks to your hands, cover and refrigerate for 10 to 20 minutes.)

4. Bake until lightly browned, 20 to 30 minutes. Let cool completely in pan on a wire rack. Using excess parchment as handles, carefully remove from pan, and place on a large cutting board.

5. In a medium bowl, whisk together confectioners' sugar, melted butter, grapefruit juice, lime juice, orange juice, and remaining ¼ teaspoon salt. Spread onto shortbread; garnish with zests, if desired. Let stand until glaze is set, about 10 minutes; cut into pieces. Store in an airtight container for up to 5 days.

JAMMY BARS

Makes 24 bars

Any flavor of berry preserves and fresh berry or blend of them you like will work in this recipe. Mix and match to your heart's desire to find your favorite combination.

- 3 cups (375 grams) all-purpose flour
- 2 teaspoons (4 grams) ground ginger
- 1 teaspoon (5 grams) baking powder
- ½ teaspoon (1.5 grams) kosher salt
- 1 cup (227 grams) unsalted butter, melted
- 1 cup (200 grams) granulated sugar
- 1 cup (220 grams) firmly packed light brown sugar
- 2 large egg yolks (37 grams), room temperature
- 1½ cups (480 grams) strawberry or raspberry preserves
- 2 cups (340 grams) fresh blueberries
- 1½ cups (255 grams) fresh raspberries

1. Preheat oven to 350°F (180°C). Line a 13x9-inch baking pan with parchment paper, letting excess extend over sides. Spray parchment with cooking spray.
2. In a large bowl, whisk together flour, ginger, baking powder, and salt.
3. In a medium bowl, whisk together melted butter, sugars, and egg yolks. Using a wooden spoon, stir butter mixture into flour mixture until well combined and crumbly.
4. Press 3 cups (490 grams) crumb mixture into bottom of prepared pan. Spread preserves onto crust, leaving a ¼-inch border around all sides. Top with berries. Sprinkle remaining crumb mixture onto berries.
5. Bake for 30 minutes. Loosely cover with foil, and bake until set, 30 to 40 minutes more. Let cool completely in pan on a wire rack.
6. Using excess parchment as handles, remove from pan before cutting into bars. Refrigerate in an airtight container for up to 3 days.

FUDGY BROWNIES

Makes about 9 brownies

Melted chocolate and butter transform the texture of these brownies into pure decadence. A boost of fat from the chocolate's cocoa butter enriches the crumb, and a touch of cocoa powder rounds out the flavor. With a glossy top, dense interior, and chewy finish, these brownies are a guaranteed crowd-pleaser.

---

8 ounces (226 grams) bittersweet chocolate, chopped
¾ cup (170 grams) unsalted butter, cubed
1 cup (200 grams) granulated sugar
¾ cup (165 grams) firmly packed dark brown sugar
1¼ cups (156 grams) all-purpose flour
3 tablespoons (15 grams) unsweetened cocoa powder, sifted
¾ teaspoon (2.25 grams) kosher salt
¾ teaspoon (1.5 grams) instant espresso powder
4 large eggs (200 grams), room temperature and beaten
2 teaspoons (8 grams) vanilla extract

1. Preheat oven to 325°F (170°C). Spray an 8-inch square baking pan with cooking spray. Line pan with parchment paper, letting excess extend over sides of pan.
2. In the top of a double boiler, combine chocolate and butter. Cook over simmering water, stirring occasionally, until melted and smooth. Turn off heat, and whisk in sugars until well combined. (Mixture will not be completely smooth.) Remove from heat, and let cool slightly, 3 to 5 minutes.
3. In a medium bowl, whisk together flour, cocoa, salt, and espresso powder.
4. Gradually whisk eggs into chocolate mixture until combined. Whisk in vanilla. Fold in flour mixture just until combined. Spread batter in prepared pan.
5. Bake until a wooden pick inserted in center comes out with a few moist crumbs, 50 to 55 minutes. Let cool in pan for 15 minutes. Using excess parchment as handles, remove from pan, and let cool completely on a wire rack before cutting into bars. Refrigerate in an airtight container for up to 5 days.

CARROT CAKE BLONDIES

Makes 9 blondies

Cake gets a conversion to chewy, buttery blondies in this decadent treat. Filled with carrots, a blend of warm spices, and crunchy chopped pecans and then slathered with frosting and sprinkled with more toasty pecans, these beautiful blondies are sure to be a crowd-pleaser.

- 1 cup plus 1 tablespoon (234 grams) firmly packed dark brown sugar
- 1 cup (227 grams) unsalted butter, melted
- 2 large eggs (100 grams), room temperature and lightly beaten
- 2 teaspoons (8 grams) vanilla extract
- 1 cup (147 grams) finely grated carrots (see Note)
- 1½ cups (188 grams) all-purpose flour
- 1 teaspoon (2 grams) ground cinnamon
- ½ teaspoon (1.5 grams) kosher salt
- ½ teaspoon (1 gram) ground ginger
- ½ cup (57 grams) chopped lightly toasted pecans
- Cream Cheese Frosting (recipe follows)
- Garnish: chopped lightly toasted pecans

1. Preheat oven to 350°F (180°C). Spray a 9-inch square baking pan with baking spray with flour. Line pan with parchment paper, letting edges extend over sides of pan.
2. In a large bowl, whisk together brown sugar, melted butter, and eggs until smooth and well combined. Whisk in vanilla. Fold in carrots.
3. In a medium bowl, whisk together flour, cinnamon, salt, and ginger. Add flour mixture to sugar mixture, and stir just until combined. Fold in pecans. Spread batter into prepared pan.
4. Bake until edges are golden brown and center is set, 32 to 35 minutes. Let cool completely in pan on a wire rack.
5. Using excess parchment as handles, remove from pan, and spread Cream Cheese Frosting on top. Garnish with pecans, if desired. Cut into bars. Refrigerate in an airtight container for up to 3 days.

Cream Cheese Frosting

Makes about 2 cups

- 8 ounces (226 grams) cream cheese, softened
- 4 cups (480 grams) confectioners' sugar
- 2 tablespoons (30 grams) heavy whipping cream

1. In the bowl of a stand mixer fitted with the paddle attachment, beat cream cheese at medium-high speed until smooth. Reduce mixer speed to medium-low, and add confectioners' sugar, 1 cup (120 grams) at a time, beating until combined and stopping to scrape sides of bowl. Add cream, and beat at medium-high speed until smooth. Use immediately.

BLACK COCOA CHEESECAKE BROWNIES

Makes 12 brownies

Chocoholics and cheesecake lovers, unite! My fudgy brownies are swirled with a luscious layer of cheesecake filling so you get plenty of creamy and tangy cheesecake in each bite.

Brownie:

2⅓ cups (397 grams) extra-dark chocolate chips
1 cup (227 grams) unsalted butter, cubed
1½ cups (300 grams) granulated sugar
1 cup (220 grams) firmly packed dark brown sugar
1½ cups (188 grams) all-purpose flour
¾ cup (64 grams) black cocoa powder
2 teaspoons (6 grams) kosher salt
5 large eggs (250 grams), beaten
1 tablespoon (13 grams) vanilla extract

Cheesecake:

2 (8-ounce) packages (454 grams) cream cheese, softened
1 cup (200 grams) granulated sugar
1 tablespoon (8 grams) all-purpose flour
2 large eggs (100 grams)
1 tablespoon (13 grams) vanilla extract

1. Preheat oven to 350°F (180°C). Spray a 13x9-inch baking pan with cooking spray. Line pan with parchment paper, letting excess extend over sides of pan.
2. For brownie: In the top of a double boiler, combine chocolate chips and butter. Cook over simmering water, stirring occasionally, until melted and smooth. Remove from heat; let mixture cool slightly. Whisk in sugars until combined.
3. In a medium bowl, whisk together flour, cocoa, and salt.
4. Gradually add beaten eggs to chocolate mixture, whisking until combined. Whisk in vanilla. Fold in flour mixture just until combined.
5. For cheesecake: In the bowl of a stand mixer fitted with the paddle attachment, beat cream cheese at medium speed until smooth. Add granulated sugar and flour; beat until combined, stopping to scrape paddle and bottom and sides of bowl. With mixer on low speed, add eggs, one at a time, beating until combined after each addition. Beat in vanilla.
6. Spread two-thirds of brownie batter into prepared pan. Dollop cheesecake mixture onto batter in pan, and gently spread smooth with an offset spatula. Dollop remaining brownie batter onto cheesecake mixture. Using a wooden pick, swirl together batter and cheesecake.
7. Bake until edges are set and an instant-read thermometer inserted in center registers 175°F (79°C) to 180°F (82°C), 50 to 55 minutes, covering with foil after 20 minutes of baking. Let cool completely in pan on a wire rack.
8. Using excess parchment as handles, remove from pan, and cut into bars. Store in an airtight container for up to 3 days.

PALLARES
SOLSONA

HAWAIIAN BARS

Makes 24 bars

Take your taste buds on a trip to the tropics with these easy bars bursting with sweet, chewy coconut and buttery, crunchy macadamia nuts.

Crust:

- 2 cups (250 grams) all-purpose flour
- 1 cup (220 grams) firmly packed light brown sugar
- 1 cup (227 grams) unsalted butter, melted
- ½ teaspoon (1.5 grams) kosher salt

Topping:

- 3 large eggs (150 grams), room temperature
- 1 (14-ounce) can (396 grams) sweetened condensed milk
- ¼ cup (55 grams) firmly packed light brown sugar
- ¼ cup (57 grams) unsalted butter, melted
- 2 tablespoons (26 grams) vanilla extract
- ½ teaspoon (1.5 grams) kosher salt
- ½ cup (63 grams) all-purpose flour
- 3 cups (252 grams) sweetened flaked coconut
- 1½ cups (170 grams) chopped macadamia nuts

1. Preheat oven to 350°F (180°C). Line a 13x9-inch baking pan with parchment paper, letting excess extend over sides of pan.

2. For crust: In a large bowl, whisk together flour, brown sugar, melted butter, and salt until combined. Press mixture into prepared pan.

3. Bake until lightly browned, 20 to 23 minutes. Let cool for 10 minutes. Reduce oven temperature to 325°F (170°C).

4. For topping: In a large bowl, whisk together eggs, condensed milk, brown sugar, melted butter, vanilla, and salt until well combined; whisk in flour. Stir in 2 cups (168 grams) coconut and macadamia nuts. Spread mixture onto prepared crust; sprinkle with remaining 1 cup (84 grams) coconut.

5. Bake until coconut is lightly browned, 30 to 35 minutes. Let cool completely in pan on a wire rack.

6. Using excess parchment as handles, remove from pan, and cut into bars. Store in an airtight container for up to 3 days.

OLD-FASHIONED BLONDIES

Makes 6 blondies

Sweet, chewy, and full of bright, citrusy flavors, these blondies remodel the classic cocktail. A thin layer of orange slices decorates the outside of the chewy base, and the inside is filled with luscious chopped cherries. Spiced with cinnamon and sweetened with light brown sugar, the full-bodied taste of whiskey is brought to new heights. Just as whiskey gets better with age, so do these small squares, as the ingredients continue to meld together the next day.

- 1 cup (220 grams) plus 2 tablespoons (28 grams) firmly packed light brown sugar, divided
- 2 medium thin-skinned oranges, such as Valencia (360 grams)
- 1 cup (125 grams) all-purpose flour
- ½ teaspoon (2.5 grams) baking powder
- ½ teaspoon (1.5 grams) kosher salt
- ½ teaspoon (1 gram) ground cinnamon
- ⅓ cup (76 grams) unsalted butter, melted and cooled
- 1 large egg (50 grams), room temperature
- 2 tablespoons (30 grams) whiskey
- 2 teaspoons (10 grams) tightly packed orange zest
- ½ teaspoon (2 grams) vanilla extract
- ¾ cup (96 grams) dried sweetened cherries, chopped

1. Preheat oven to 350°F (180°C). Spray a 9x5-inch loaf pan with baking spray with flour. Line pan with parchment paper, letting excess extend over sides of pan; spray parchment.

2. Sprinkle 2 tablespoons (28 grams) brown sugar in an even layer on bottom of prepared pan.

3. Slice each orange into 8 thin rounds (about ⅛ inch thick). Layer slices along bottom of prepared pan, overlapping as desired.

4. In a medium bowl, whisk together flour, baking powder, salt, and cinnamon.

5. In a large bowl, whisk together melted butter and remaining 1 cup (220 grams) brown sugar. Add egg, whiskey, orange zest, and vanilla, and whisk until combined. Whisk in flour mixture until almost combined. Stir in cherries until well combined and no dry spots remain. Gently spread batter onto orange slices in pan.

6. Bake until edges are golden and start to pull away from pan and a wooden pick inserted in center comes out clean, 45 to 50 minutes. Let cool in pan for 10 minutes. Invert blondie onto a wire rack, and let cool completely. Store in an airtight container for up to 3 days.

INDEX

CATEGORY

Bars
Confetti Bars, 160
Hawaiian Bars, 191
Jammy Bars, 183
Lemon Crumb Bars, 179
Triple-Citrus Sheet Pan Shortbread, 180

Blondies and Brownies
Black Cocoa Cheesecake Brownies, 188
Carrot Cake Blondies, 187
Fudgy Brownies, 184
Old-Fashioned Blondies, 192

Breads, Savory Quick
Apple-Cheddar-Sage Biscuits, 76
Chèvre and Herb Quick Bread, 80
Dill-Sour Cream-Potato Scones, 100
Mexican Street Corn Bread with Lime Butter, 79
Rosemary-Parmesan Soda Bread, 104
Upside-Down Heirloom Tomato Cornbread, 111

Breads, Sweet Quick
Cinnamon Crunch Banana Bread, 108
Cinnamon-Sugar Popovers with Peach Compote, 92
Hummingbird Scones, 95
Jumbo Blueberry-Cornmeal Muffins, 88
Key Lime Doughnuts, 87
Pumpkin-Chocolate Swirl Bread, 96
Pumpkin Snickerdoodle Muffins, 107
Spiced Apple Scones, 91
Vanilla Bean and Cardamom Scones, 116

Breads, Yeast
Angel Biscuits, 119
Babà Rustico, 99
English Muffin Loaf, 75
Fresh Corn Muffins, 115
Gluten-Free Tomato and Leek Focaccia, 83
Honey-Butter Yeast Rolls, 103
Seeded Lavash, 84
Summer Herb Dinner Rolls, 112

Buttercreams and Frostings
Chocolate Buttercream, 28
Cream Cheese Frosting, 187
Peanut Butter Frosting, 66
Spiced Cream Cheese Frosting, 55
Vanilla Bean Frosting, 58
Whipped Ricotta Frosting, 48

Cakes, Bundt and Tube
Cinnamon Blueberry Bundt Cake, 20
Cinnamon Swirl Bundt, 47
Citrus Chiffon Cake, 62
Classic Vanilla Pound Cake, 56
Coffee and Cream Marbled Coffee Cake, 27

Cakes, Loaf and Square
Confetti Snack Cake, 36
Irish Coffee Coffee Cake, 44
Pear Fritter Loaf Cake, 51
Sweet Potato Spice Cake with Toasted Meringue, 31
Sticky Toffee Pudding, 32

Cakes, Round
Apricot-Almond Streusel Kuchen, 23
Carrot-Pumpkin Cake, 55
Honey-Almond Cake, 52
Mango Sour Cream Cake, 35
Mixed Berry Ricotta Cake, 40
Raspberry Olive Oil Cake, 43
Sicilian Whole Orange Cake, 39
Stir-Together Chocolate Cake with Chocolate Buttercream, 28
Strawberry Cream Cake, 65
Torta di Susine, 61
Turtle Coffee Cake, 19
Vanilla Applesauce Cake, 58

Cakes, Sheet
Cannoli Sheet Cake, 48
Dark Chocolate Sheet Cake with Peanut Butter Frosting, 66
Marble Sheet Cake, 69

Cakes, Upside-Down
Mini Pineapple Upside-Down Cakes, 70
Peanut Butter-Banana Upside-Down Cake, 24

Condiments and Sauces
Lime Butter, 79
Peach Compote, 92
Quick Strawberry Jam, 159
Toffee Sauce, 32

Cookies
Apple-Streusel Cookies, 171
Black-and-White Cookies, 163
Chewy Chocolate Chip Cookies, 164
Chocolate-Almond Biscotti, 156
Grape Jelly-Stuffed Peanut Butter Cookies, 168
Sage, Asiago, and Pecan Shortbread Coins, 176
Snickerdoodles, 172
Soft Amaretti Cookies, 175
Strawberry Pretzel Thumbprint Cookies, 159
White Chocolate-Fruity Cereal Cookies, 167

Crusts and Doughs
All-Butter Pie Dough, 134
Crostata Dough, 137
Cheesy Crust, 153
Chocolate Chip Cookie Crust, 146
Hand Pie Dough, 141
Pecan Piecrust, 130
Pine Nut Crust, 122
Thyme Pie Dough, 142

Fillings
Almond Pastry Cream, 129
Ganache, 141
Peanut Butter Filling, 141
Raspberry Filling, 45

Glazes and Toppings
Buttermilk Glaze, 20
Chocolate Ganache, 163
Chocolate Streusel, 19
Cinnamon Sugar Topping, 108

Citrus Glaze, 62
Confetti Streusel, 36
Cream Cheese Glaze, 159
Creamy Milk Glaze, 47
Espresso Streusel, 27
Irish Whiskey Streusel, 44
Oat Streusel, 171
Snickerdoodle Streusel, 107
Spiced Glaze, 171
Swiss Meringue, 31
Vanilla Bean Meringue, 150
Vanilla Cream Cheese Glaze, 95
Vanilla Glaze, 51, 163
Whipped Mascarpone Topping, 65

Pies and Tarts, Savory
Caramelized Onion and Potato Galette, 142
Creamy Spinach Galette, 153
Heirloom Tomato and Apricot Tart, 122
Spanakopita, 125

Pies and Tarts, Sweet
Apple Crumb Pie, 145
Apricot Frangipane Tart, 129
Baked Lemon Curd Hand Pies, 141
Bougatsa, 149
Brookie Pie, 146
Chocolate-Toffee Pecan Pie, 130
Honey Pie, 126
Peach, Blackberry, and Bourbon Crostata, 137
Pear and Honeyed Goat Cheese Galette, 133
Peanut Butter Pie, 138
Stone Fruit Galette, 134
Sweet Potato Tart, 150

FLAVOR/ INGREDIENT

Cheese
Apple-Cheddar-Sage Biscuits, 76
Babà Rustico, 99
Chèvre and Herb Quick Bread, 80
Creamy Spinach Galette, 153
Mascarpone-Ricotta Tart, 143
Mexican Street Corn Bread with Lime Butter, 79
Pear and Honeyed Goat Cheese Galette, 133
Rosemary-Parmesan Soda Bread, 104
Sage, Asiago, and Pecan Shortbread Coins, 176
Upside-Down Heirloom Tomato Cornbread, 111

Chocolate
Black-and-White Cookies, 163
Black Cocoa Cheesecake Brownies, 188
Brookie Pie, 146
Cannoli Sheet Cake, 48
Chewy Chocolate Chip Cookies, 164
Chocolate-Almond Biscotti, 156
Chocolate-Toffee Pecan Pie, 130
Dark Chocolate Sheet Cake with Peanut Butter Frosting, 66
Fudgy Brownies, 184
Marble Sheet Cake, 69
Peanut Butter Pie, 138
Pumpkin-Chocolate Swirl Bread, 94
Stir-Together Chocolate Cake with Chocolate Buttercream, 28
Turtle Coffee Cake, 19
White Chocolate-Fruity Cereal Cookies, 167

Citrus
Baked Lemon Curd Hand Pies, 148
Citrus Chiffon Cake, 62
Key Lime Doughnuts, 87
Lemon Crumb Bars, 179
Old-Fashioned Blondies, 192
Sicilian Whole Orange Cake, 39
Triple-Citrus Sheet Pan Shortbread, 180

Coffee
Coffee and Cream Marble Coffee Cake, 27
Irish Coffee Coffee Cake, 44

Fruit
Apple-Cheddar-Sage Biscuits, 76
Apple Crumb Pie, 145
Apple-Streusel Cookies, 171
Apricot-Almond Streusel Kuchen, 23
Apricot Frangipane Tart, 129
Cinnamon Blueberry Bundt Cake, 20
Cinnamon Crunch Banana Bread, 108
Cinnamon-Sugar Popovers with Peach Compote, 92
Grape Jelly-Stuffed Peanut Butter Cookies, 168
Heirloom Tomato and Apricot Tart, 122
Hummingbird Scones, 95
Jammy Bars, 183
Jumbo Blueberry Cornmeal Muffins, 88
Mango Sour Cream Cake, 35
Mini Pineapple Upside-Down Cakes, 70
Mixed Berry Ricotta Cake, 40
Peach, Blackberry, and Bourbon Crostata, 137
Peanut Butter-Banana Upside-Down Cake, 24
Pear and Honeyed Goat Cheese Galette, 133
Pear Fritter Loaf Cake, 51
Raspberry Olive Oil Cake, 43
Spiced Apple Scones, 91
Sticky Toffee Pudding, 32
Stone Fruit Galette, 134
Strawberry Cream Cake, 65
Strawberry Pretzel Thumbprint Cookies, 159
Torta di Susine, 61
White Chocolate-Fruity Cereal Cookies, 167

Herbs
Caramelized Onion and Potato Galette, 142
Chèvre and Herb Quick Bread, 80
Dill-Sour Cream-Potato Scones, 100
Rosemary-Parmesan Soda Bread, 104
Sage, Asiago, and Pecan Shortbread Coins, 176
Seeded Lavash, 84
Spanakopita, 125
Summer Herb Dinner Rolls, 112
Upside-Down Heirloom Tomato Cornbread, 111

Honey

Honey-Almond Cake, 52
Honey-Butter Yeast Rolls, 103
Honey Pie, 130
Pear and Honeyed Goat Cheese Galette, 134

Nuts and Seeds

Apricot-Almond Streusel Kuchen, 23
Apricot Frangipane Tart, 129
Cannoli Sheet Cake, 48
Carrot Cake Blondies, 187
Chocolate-Almond Biscotti, 156
Chocolate-Toffee Pecan Pie, 130
Grape Jelly-Stuffed Peanut Butter Cookies, 168
Hawaiian Bars, 191
Honey-Almond Cake, 52
Peanut Butter-Banana Upside-Down Cake, 24
Peanut Butter Pie, 138
Sage, Asiago, and Pecan Shortbread Coins, 176
Seeded Lavash, 84
Soft Amaretti Cookies, 175
Turtle Coffee Cake, 19

Spices

Bougatsa, 149
Carrot Cake Blondies, 187
Carrot-Pumpkin Cake, 55
Cinnamon Crunch Banana Bread, 108
Cinnamon Swirl Bundt, 47
Pumpkin Snickerdoodle Muffins, 107
Snickerdoodles, 172
Spiced Apple Scones, 91
Sticky Toffee Pudding, 32
Sweet Potato Spice Cake with Toasted Meringue, 31
Sweet Potato Tart, 150
Vanilla Bean and Cardamom Scones, 116

Vanilla

Black-and-White Cookies, 163
Black Cocoa Cheesecake Brownies, 188
Bougatsa, 149
Classic Vanilla Pound Cake, 56
Confetti Bars, 160
Confetti Snack Cake, 34
Vanilla Applesauce Cake, 58
Vanilla Bean and Cardamom Scones, 116

Vegetables

Caramelized Onion and Potato Galette, 142
Carrot Cake Blondies, 187
Carrot-Pumpkin Cake, 55
Creamy Spinach Galette, 153
Dill-Sour Cream-Potato Scones, 100
Fresh Corn Muffins, 115
Gluten-Free Tomato and Leek Focaccia, 83
Heirloom Tomato and Apricot Tart, 122
Mexican Street Corn Bread with Lime Butter, 79
Spanakopita, 125
Sweet Potato Spice Cake with Toasted Meringue, 31
Sweet Potato Tart, 150
Upside-Down Heirloom Tomato Cornbread, 111

CREDITS

Editor-in-Chief Brian Hart Hoffman
EVP/Chief Content Officer Brooke Michael Bell
Editorial Director Nancy Meeks
Art Director Liz Kight
Graphic Designer Kile Pointer
Associate Editor Amber Wilson
Assistant Editor Christina Fleisch
Senior Copy Editor Meg Lundberg
Senior Digital Imaging Specialist Delisa McDaniel

Test Kitchen Director Laura Crandall
Recipe Developers/Food Stylists Ola Agbodza, Aaron Conrad, Katie Moon Dickerson, Amanda Stabile
Contributing Recipe Developer Jessie Sheehan

Senior Stylist Sidney Bragiel
Stylists Maghan Armstrong, Courtni Bodiford, Maggie Hill
Contributing Stylists Lucy Finney, Mary Beth Jones

Photographers Jim Bathie, Kyle Carpenter, John O'Hagan, Stephanie Welbourne Steele
Contributing Photographer Mac Jamieson

Cover
Photography by Kyle Carpenter
Recipe Development and Food Styling by Katie Moon Dickerson
Styling by Maggie Hill

about the author

A former flight attendant and self-taught baker, Brian Hart Hoffman spent his early life traveling and discovering bakeries around the world, returning home with a mission to re-create the recipes. Brian launched an award-winning brand dedicated to the celebration of the global baking community: *Bake from Scratch*. Now, *Bake from Scratch* is one of the world's largest baking platforms, with magazines and best-selling cookbooks, a podcast (*The Crumb*), sell-out international and domestic baking retreats, and, of course, @thebakefeed on Instagram, a way for bakers around the world to connect.

Brian has authored numerous best-selling books, including *The Coupe*, *Holiday Coupetails*, *The Bread Collection*, *The Pie & Tart Collection*, *The Cake Collection*, *The Cookie Collection*, *Holiday Cookies*, and *Bake from Scratch: Artisan Recipes for the Home Baker* volumes 1, 2, 3, 4, 5, 6, 7, and 8.